D1055469

POEMS FROM BLACK AFRICA

edited by Langston Hughes

ETHIOPIA

SOUTH RHODESIA

SIERRA LEONE

MADAGASCAR

IVORY COAST

NIGERIA

KENYA

Poems from Black Africa

GABON

SENEGAL

NYASALAND

MOZAMBIQUE

SOUTH AFRICA

CONGO | GHANA

LIBERIA

Indiana University Press
BLOOMINGTON & LONDON

UNESCO COLLECTION OF CONTEMPORARY WORKS

This volume has been accepted in the Translations Series of Contemporary Works jointly sponsored by the International PEN Club and the United Nations Educational, Scientific and Cultural Organization (UNESCO).

THIRD PRINTING 1967

See page 159 for detailed acknowledgments

Library of Congress Catalog Card Number 62-8972

First Midland Book Edition 1966

Manufactured in the United States of America

Decorations from printed fabric, Abeokuto, Nigeria (Indiana University Fine Arts Collection)

to

PETER ABRAHAMS

of

SOUTH AFRICA

Acknowledgments

LANGSTON HUGHES wishes to thank the following persons for their aid in assembling the poems in this volume and, in some cases, for invaluable assistance in editing, translating, or the gathering of biographical notes: Francis Ernest Kobina Parkes, Dr. A. C. Jordan, Roland Tombekai Dempster; Ulli Beier, co-editor of *Black Orpheus;* Peggy Rutherfoord, editor of *Darkness and Light;* the editors and publishers of *Drum;* Dr. Hugh Smythe, George Bass; as well as many of the poets herein for informing other poets of my search for indigenous poetry.

Contents

Ghana

Liberia

Nigeria

Translators' names appear at the ends of poems.

Foreword by Langston Hughes

USUALLY poets have their fingers on the emotional pulse of their peoples, of their homelands. Traditionally, poets are lyric historians. From the days of the bards and troubadours, the songs of the poets have been not only songs, but often *records* of the most moving events, the deepest thoughts and most profound emotional currents of their times. To understand Africa today, it is wise to listen to what its poets say—those who put their songs down on paper as well as those who only speak or sing them. Perhaps it is more profitable to know how people *feel* than it is to know what they think. Certainly the poetry of contemporary Africa indicates its emotional climate. That climate is one of hope and of faith in a future that is coming more and more into the control of the peoples of Africa themselves.

But the best of the black poets writing today in English or French in Africa South of the Sahara are not so much propagandists for African nationalism, as they are spokesmen for variations of *négritude*—a word the French-speaking writers have coined to express a pride in and a love of the African heritage, physically, spiritually and culturally. The most interesting non-white poets of contemporary Africa are modernists in style, in contrast to the older writers of colonial days who were influenced by Victorian models or by the classical French poets taught in the missionary schools. Contemporary young African intellectuals, some of whom have but lately come home from Cambridge or the Sorbonne, are not unlike young writers elsewhere. They have read Auden and Spender and Eliot, Mauriac, Jacques Prevert and perhaps Brecht. Lagos, Accra or Dakar are no longer weeks away from Europe. In fact, from the heart of Africa to Paris or London by jet is now only a matter of hours. Not that all African writers have traveled abroad. But the bookshops in Africa's major cities today are fairly well stocked. Even American books make their way to the West Coast and the Union of South Africa. Then there is the BBC—the African networks of the British Broadcasting Company beaming from London cultural programs of high calibre and using much more poetry than the American airwaves ever dream of committing to the microphones. Many young African writers today augment their incomes by writing for BBC, which pays not badly for both poetry and prose.

Whatever their influences may be, local or foreign, there are sensitive and exciting poets in Black Africa now. Abioseh Nicol in Sierra Leone, Kobina Parkes in Ghana, Gabriel Okara in Nigeria, Sédar-Senghor of Senegal, Ezekiel Mphahlele of South Africa to name men who have produced more than simply an occasional magazine or newspaper verse. These poets represent their countries well on the printed page, and all of them have lately been published abroad as well as at home. The poetry of Abioseh Nicol is quietly moving and deeply personal; that of Kobina Parkes kaleidoscopically vivid and almost tribal in its imagery; while Okara's is sensitive and strange and semi-mystic to the Western reader. In the work of Dennis Osadebay and Michael Dei-Anang the poet and pamphleteer meet to cry aloud for African freedom, while in Senghor's poems of *négritude* French sophistication and the tall drums of Senegal lock arms.

In general the French African poets, and particularly Senghor, tend toward creating Whitmanesque catalogues of fruits, rivers, trees and the other physical attributes of their land, and vie with one another in evoking the strength of black bodies, the dignity of black motherhood, the beauty of black maidens. From Senghor's *Femme Noire:*

Naked woman, dark woman,
Ripe fruit with firm flesh,
Sombre ecstasy of dark red wine,
Mouth which makes mine lyrical. . . .

The French poets of color create mosaics of blackness against the palm trees within a large and (to non-Africans) exotic framework of cultural nationalism, seldom tending toward miniatures, seldom reducing their subject matter to the framework of oneself. Black poets writing in English-speaking Africa, on the other hand, seem somewhat less concerned with color, personal or in landscape, and are more centered in self rather than race, their *I* less the *I* equivalent to *We* of the French poets. But the best poetry of both French and English expression bears the stamp of the African personality, and most of its emotional aura might be included within the term *négritude*—that "anti-racist racism," as Sartre called it, of black Africa's concentration on the rediscovery of self, a turning within for values to live by, rather than a striking outward in revenge for past wrongs. "Me fait songer à Orphée allant réclamer Eurydice à Pluton," wrote Sartre in his famous introduction to Senghor's anthology of French African poetry.

In a paper on African literature delivered at the First International Congress of Africanists at the University of Ghana, Ezekiel Mphahlele confirms that in general, "English and French writing move along different tracks, particularly in the realm of poetry. The Nigerian poet talks about things as they affect him personally and immediately. He is not protesting or trying to vindicate his blackness. The French-speaking poet, however, particularly of the *négritude* school, uses broad symbols in which immediacy of individual experience is not the important thing. These are symbols of Africa, of blackness, of what is regarded by the poet as African traits which are expected to be a unifying force—not only for the indigenous people of the continent but for the Negro world in general."

The American Negro poet, Samuel Allen (Paul Vesey) writing on *négritude* says, "It represents in one sense the Negro African poet's endeavor to recover for his race a normal self-pride, a confidence in himself shattered for centuries when the enslaver suddenly loomed in the village pathway; to recover a world in which he once again could have a sense of unashamed identity and an unsubordinate role. . . . *Négritude* includes the characteristic impulses, traits and habits which may be considered more markedly Negro African than white or European. It is thus something which the poet possesses in the wells of his being and simultaneously something which he is seeking to recover, to make manifest; and again it is a subjective disposition which is affirmed and which objectivizes itself in the poem."

Most of the poems of Léopold Sédar-Senghor are colored by the blackness of Africa. The titles of his various works indicate as much: *Chants d'Ombres, Masque Negre, Hosties Noires, A l'Appel de la Race de Saba*, among others. He sings of the glories of blackness, of Africa's past trials and tribulations and of its future glories. Concerning his style, really that of a chant, Senghor writes, "I insist that the poem is perfect only when it becomes a song: words and music at once. It is time to stop the decay of the modern world and especially the decay of poetry. Poetry must find its way back to its origins, to the times when it was sung and danced. As it was in Greece, above all in the Egypt of the Pharaohs. And as it is still today in black Africa."

Certainly many indigenous poets in contemporary Africa, whether writing in the *lingua franca* of English or French, are still close enough to tribal life to know the names of the old non-Christian gods, the *orisha*, to hear in their ears the great mass chants of ancient rituals or the jolly rhymes of village feasts. Oral poetry is very much a part of daily living in tribal Africa where art and life have not yet parted company. The bulk of Africa's poetry is still that which is only spoken or sung. Most of it is not yet transcribed or translated into European tongues, and much of it is closely related to music, the rhythms of percussion and the dance, and is concerned with community rituals and the traditional gods worshipped by non-Christian or non-Moslem peoples.

Since oral poetry is highly regional, often with allusions and overtones obscure beyond tribal limits, much traditional verse is almost untranslatable. Then, too, like the Chinese, many tribal tongues utilize tone and pitch as well as mere words in communication. One example is the Yoruba of Nigeria. With them the same word pronounced in one tone may have quite a different meaning in another tone or inflection. There have been many adequate translations into English of African folk tales, the story line remaining intact. To translate folk poetry is, however, a much more formidable task. Ulli Beier of the University College at Ibadan is one of the few Europeans doing extensive work in this field. It is a privilege to include in this book some of Beier's translations from the Yoruba.

There will no doubt arise in the New Africa creative writers who will soon combine in poetry the written word and the oral traditionals of the bush as excitingly as Amos Tutuola of *The Palm Wine Drinkard* has combined English prose and tribal lore in fiction. Certainly this integration of indigenous elements can be beautifully done in poetry, as Nicolás Guillén of Cuba has proven in his poems of *ñañigo* and his use of the rhythms of *sones*. Written poetry in Africa today is moving away from the bench of the missionary school to walk abroad beneath the cocoa palms and listen for inspiration to the native songs in many tongues. Soon African poetry will capture the essence of these songs and recreate them on paper. Meanwhile, it walks with grace and already is beginning to achieve an individuality quite its own.

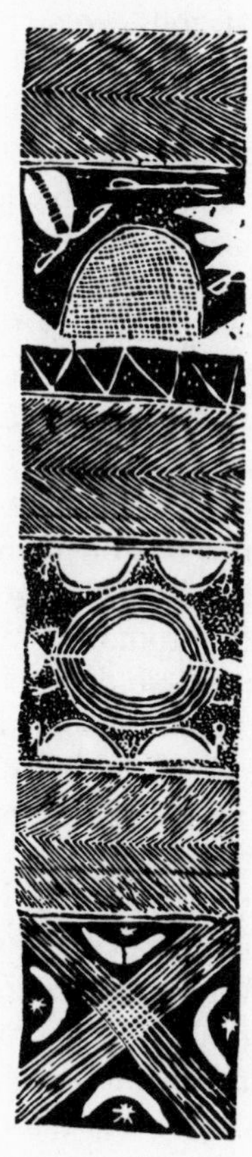

YORUBA

BANTU

KRU

MADAGASCAR

BAULE

IBO

Oral Traditionals

AKAN

GABON

FANTI

HLUBI

XHOSA

JOHANNESBURG

ZEZURU

AMHARIC

Yoruba [Nigeria]

THREE FRIENDS

I had three friends.
One asked me to sleep on the mat.
One asked me to sleep on the ground.
One asked me to sleep on his breast.
I decided to sleep on his breast.
I saw myself carried on a river.
I saw the king of the river
And the king of the sun.
There in that country I saw palm trees
So weighed down with fruit
That the trees bent under the fruit,
And fruit killed them.

ULLI BEIER

ORIKI ERINLE

He is firm and strong
like an ancient rock.
He is clear like the eye of god

that does not grow any grass.
Like the earth he will never change.
He puts out the lamp
and lets his eye sparkle like fire.
He will turn the barren woman
into one who carries child.
He is the father of our king.
He is the one who looks after my child.

ULLI BEIER

ERIN (ELEPHANT)

Elephant who brings death.
Elephant, a spirit in the bush.
With his single hand
He can pull two palm trees to the ground.
If he had two hands
He would tear the heavens like an old rag.
The spirit who eats dog,
The spirit who eats ram,
The spirit who eats
A whole palm fruit with its thorns.
With his four mortal legs
He tramples down the grass.
Wherever he walks,
The grass is forbidden to stand up again.
An elephant is not a load for an old man—
Nor for a young man either.

ULLI BEIER

SHANGO

Shango is an animal like the gorilla.
A rare animal in the forest.
As rare as the monkey who is a medicine man.
Shango, do not give me a little of your medicine,
Give me all! So that I can spread it over my face and mouth.
Anybody who waits for the elephant, waits for death.
Anybody who waits for the buffalo, waits for death.
Anybody who waits for the railway, waits for trouble.
He says we must avoid the thing that will kill us.
He says we must avoid trouble.
He is the one who waited for the things we are running
away from.

He kneels down, like a collector of vegetables.
Shango does not collect vegetables,
He is only looking for the head of the farmer.
The farmer was deceived.
He went to the farm, only to be killed.
My lord do not sacrifice me to your inner being.

I will not regard anybody but you in my life.
Shango I beg you, let my life be good.
I want what is in your hand.
I want a good thing from you.
Give me my own present today.
I will regard you alone.
I beg, I beg, I have nobody except you.
Do not fight me.
Give me my own child.

ULLI BEIER

HUNGER

Hunger makes a person climb up to the ceiling
And hold on to the rafters.
It makes a person lie down—
But not feel at rest.
It makes a person lie down—
Unable to stand.
It makes a person lie down—
And count the rafters.
When the Moslem is not hungry, he says:
We are forbidden to eat monkey.
When Ibrahim is hungry he eats a baboon!
When hunger beats the woman in the harem,
She will run out into the street in daytime.
One who is hungry does not care for taboos.
One who is hungry does not care for death.
One who is hungry will take
Out of the sacrifice money.
When death shuts the door,
Hunger will open it.
"I have filled my belly yesterday"
Does not concern hunger.
There is no God like one's throat.
We have to sacrifice daily to it.

ULLI BEIER

Bantu [Congo]

PADDLING SONG

My dugout canoe goes
Swiftly down the river.
In every tree the monkeys

Are chattering and crying.
Oh, big jungle hunter,
Tell me of their trouble.

The little monkey broke his leg,
So they all are crying.

Then bend to your paddle,
Hunter of the river,
And tell the mother that
Her monkey-baby's crying:
The little monkey broke his leg.
They are all crying.

MAX EXNER

Kru [Liberia]

NANA KRU

Nana, Nana Kru,
Jump in my canoe.
Nana, I paid
My dowry for you.

I saw your ma
And I saw your pa.
I gave them two goat,
Two cow, sixteen sheep.

Jump in my canoe.
Nana, I paid
My dowry for you,
Nana, Nana Kru.

as sung by R. VAN RICHARDS

Folk Song [Madagascar]

HALF SIGH

Half sigh imaginary flower,
The girl had come to meet me
When it occurred to her parents to stop her.
I addressed her with beautiful words
But she did not answer. . . .

You will get old here,
You and remorse.
We and love,
We shall go home.

MIRIAM KOSHLAND

Baule [Ivory Coast]

THE SORROW OF KODIO

We were three women, three men
And myself, Kodio Ango.
We were on our way to work in the city
And I lost my wife, Nanama, on the way.
I alone have lost my wife,
To me alone such misery has happened,
To me alone, Kodio,
The most handsome of the three men,
Such misery has happened.
In vain I call for my wife.
She died on the way like a chicken running.

How shall I tell her mother?
How shall I tell it to her, I Kodio,
When it is so hard
To hold back my own pain?

MIRIAM KOSHLAND

Ibo [Nigeria]

O LAMB GIVE ME MY SALT

O lamb give me my salt,
Salt the market folk gave me;
The market folk ate my fruits,
Fruits the fruit picker gave me;
The farmer broke my hoe,
Hoe the smith gave me;
The smith ate my yam
Yam an old woman gave me;
The old woman ate my bird,
The bird my trap gave me,
My faithful, useful trap.

DENNIS C. OSADEBAY

Akan [Ghana]

FOOLISH CHILD

My mother bore me,
A foolish child,
Whirr, whirr!

Father begat me,
A foolish child.
  Whirr, whirr!

My mother bore me,
A simpleton.
  Whirr, whirr!

Father begat me,
A simpleton.
  Whirr, whirr!

J. B. DANQUAH

Folk Song [Gabon]

THE LITTLE BIRD

One morning I got up
to pick oranges in the garden.
And I saw this.
I saw the rising sun
and the little bird
singing his morning song.
And I heard this.
The little bird chirped: "Cui, cui, cui!"
And begged:
"Please, leave my little ones in their nest."
And I said this:
First I chirped: "Cui, cui, cui!"
And then I said:
"Don't be afraid, I am your friend."
And what was asked I did.

Since that day the little bird loves me
and his sweet song gives me great pleasure.
And this is what happened.

ROLF ITALIAANDER

Fanti [Ghana]

PRAYER FOR EVERY DAY

Almighty and everlasting God, we thank Thee.
Thou art likened to the Corona constellation
Which makes the warm sea icy:
The bright rays of the sun
That reach the darkest spot in the forest;
The stumpy tree in the road
Over which only the wise can go;
The egg from which no one can tie a knot.
Thou bird of the roadway!
Thou guide of the dead!
The single creeper that constitutes the grove!
The ring on the father's finger!
The deep water whose bed no one has seen!
The vigilant that can trace
The footmarks of the duiker on the rock!
The lion of Eminsa grove!
Blessings be unto Thee!

KWEKU MARTIN

Hlubi [South Africa]

SHAKA, KING OF THE ZULUS

He is Shaka the unshakable,
Thunderer-while-sitting, son of Menzi.
He is the bird that preys on other birds,
The battle-axe that excels other battle-axes.
He is the long-strided-pursuer, son of Ndaba,
Who pursued the moon and the sun.
He is a great hubbub like the rocks of Nkandla
Where the elephants take shelter
When the heavens frown.
'Tis he whose spears resound causing wailings,
Thus old women shall stay in abandoned homes,
And old men shall drop by the wayside.

A. C. JORDAN

Xhosa [South Africa]

THOU GREAT GOD

Thou great God that dwellest in Heaven,
Thou are the shield, the stronghold of truth.
'Tis Thou, and Thou alone, that dwellest in the highest,
Thou the maker of life and the skies,
Thou the maker of the sparse and clustered stars,
As the shooting-star doth proclaim.
The horn soundeth aloud, calling us
To Thee, great Hunter, Hunter of souls,
Who maketh one herd of friend and foe,

All covered and sheltered under Thy cloak.
Thou are the little Lamb, Mesiyas,
Whose hands are wounded with nailing,
Thy blood that streameth for ever and ever
For the sake of us men was shed.

A. C. JORDAN

ABSENT LOVER

The far-off mountains hide you from me,
While the nearer ones overhang me;
Would that I had a heavy sledge
To crush the mountains near me;
Would that I had wings like a bird
To fly over those farther away.

A. C. JORDAN

SIX TO SIX

A mighty bell is six o'clock.
I went to Rhini and found the men
Driven by six o'clock;
I went to Qonce and found the men
Toiling at six o'clock;
Back at Tinarha I found the men
Bullied by six o'clock.

A. C. JORDAN

Johannesburg [South Africa]

PASS OFFICE SONG

The scene is any pass office, where all male Africans must go to get their Registration Certificates. There they may wait in queues for hours and sometimes for days before they are attended to. It is a regulation which rankles in their minds and so they sing about it.

Take off your hat.
What is your home name?
Who is your father?
Who is your chief?
Where do you pay your tax?
What river do you drink?
We mourn for our country.

transcribed by PEGGY RUTHERFOORD

Zezuru [South Rhodesia]

KEEP IT DARK

Keep it dark!
Don't tell your wife,
For your wife is a log
That is smouldering surely!
Keep it dark!

Keep it dark!
Don't tell your wife,

For your wife is a pot—
And then "Bang!"
It's all out and about!
Keep it dark!

HUGH TRACEY

Amharic [Ethiopia]

TROUSERS OF WIND

A household song about a worthless lover, sung by women as they work.

Trousers of wind and buttons of hail;
A lump of Shoa earth, at Gondar nothing left;
A hyena bearing meat, led by a leather thong;
Some water in a glass left standing by the fire;
A measure of water thrown on the hearth;
A horse of mist and a swollen ford;
Useless for anything, useful to no one;
Why am I in love with such a man as he?

SYLVIA PANKHURST
assisted by Ato Menghestu Lemme

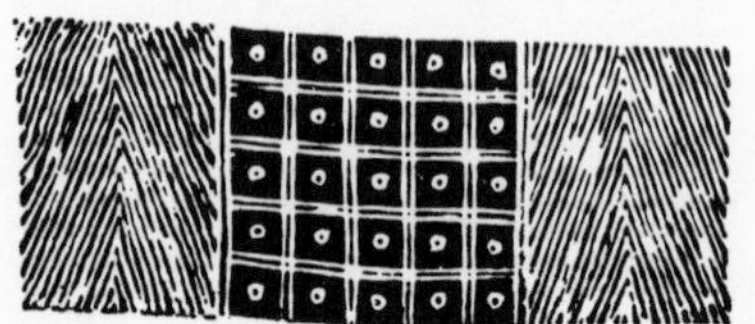

SIERRA LEONE

NYASALAND

English-speaking Poets

LIBERIA

KENYA

NIGERIA

SOUTH AFRICA

GHANA

SIERRA LEONE

Abioseh Nicol

AFRICAN EASTER

I *Good Friday*

THE WOUNDED CHRIST:

I am not your God
If you have not denied me once, twice,
If I have not heard you complaining,
Or doubting my existence.

I am not your Love,
If you have not rejected me often.
For what then am I worth to you
If you are always sinless.

Pace these sandy corridors of time,
Turn again and live for me your youth, listening
To the gently falling rain, the distant cock crow
Then proceed once more to deny

That I had a part in your being. Say
That I am an invention to keep you held

Always in thralldom. That I was
The avant-garde of your disintegration.

After me, the stone jars of cheap gin, the ornamental
Glass beads, the punitive expeditions, your colonial status,
I have heard it all before; hide your face,
Bury it, for fear that finding me, you may find peace.

For in this hour when the dying night lingers
Unwilling to surrender its wakening darkness
Over your face and fevered brow, my torn fingers
Will stray bringing such comfort
As may calm your doubting heart

II *Easter Eve*

THE AFRICAN PRIEST:

I have sat me down by the waterside
Watching the grey river pulling away.
I have listened me with willing ears
To your vesper bells across the fields.

Come close to me, God, do not keep away,
I walk towards you but you are too far,
Please try and meet me here halfway,
Because you are my all, my all.

What are you, Negro, Lebanese or Jew,
Flemish, Italian, Indian, Greek?
I know within my heart exactly what you are—
What we would like to be, but never are.

The warm blood sticks to your whipped shoulders
(Drink this in remembrance of me).
Only when the whirling thongs have raised the red weals
On our complacent bodies, then we remember you.
Change our salty tears of brown remorse

Into your flowing blood, it tastes the same.
(Oh, River Niger, you too have come from far away),
Fill my uplifted silver calabash
With your new sacrificial wine.

And I, your least novitiate, will sip,
With my thick lips, your ancient memory.
So God the Father who art above,
Christ His Son, our only love,
Holy Ghost, eternal Dove,
Make of me a goodly man.

III *Easter Morning*

THE AFRICAN INTELLECTUAL:

Ding dong bell
Pussy's in the well.

Another day . . .

Sleep leaves my opening eyes slowly
Unwillingly like a true lover.

But this day is different.
The lonely matin bells
Cut across the thin morning mist,
The glinting dew on the green grass,
The cool pink light before the heat of day,
The sudden punctual dawn of tropic skies,
Before the muezzin begins to cry,
Before the pagan drums begin to beat.

Easter morning.

But still for me
The great rock remains unrolled.

Within my wet dark tomb
Wounded peace remains embalmed,
The pricking thorns still yet my crown.

Easter morning.

Where are my ancestral spirits now?
I have forgotten for many harvests
To moisten the warm earth
With poured libations.
Where are you now, O Shango?
Two-headed, powerful
Man and woman, hermaphrodite
Holding your quivering thunderbolts
With quiet savage malice;
Brooding over your domain,
Africa, Cuba, Haiti, Brazil,
Slavery of mind is unabolished.
Always wanting to punish, never to love.

I have turned away from you
To One who stands
Watching His dying dispossessed Son
Shouting in Aramaic agony
Watching the white Picasso dove
Hovering above the Palestinian stream
Watching and waiting, sometimes
To punish, always to love.

Sleep confuses my tired mind.
Still the bell rings
I must up and away.
I am a good Churchman, now.
Broadminded, which means past caring,
Whether High or Low.
The priest may hold the chalice,

Or give it to me. It depends
On where he trained. I only mind
That he wipes the wet rim
Not to spread dental germs.
A tenth of my goods
I give to the poor
Through income tax.

Easter morning.

Yet You Christ are always there.
You are the many-faceted crystal
Of our desires and hopes,
Behind the smoke-screen of incense,
Concealed in mumbled European tongues
Of worship and of praise.
In the thick dusty verbiage
Of centuries of committees
Of ecumenical councils.
You yet remain revealed
To those who seek you.
It is I, you say.
You remain in the sepulchre
Of my brown body.

Christ is risen, Christ is risen!

You were not dead.
It was just that we
Could not see clearly enough.
We can push out the rock from the inside.
You can come out now.
You see we want to share you
With our masters, because
You really are unique.

The great muddy river Niger,
Picks up the rising equatorial sun,
Changing itself by slow degrees
Into thick flowing molten gold.

THE MEANING OF AFRICA

Africa, you were once just a name to me
But now you lie before me with sombre green challenge
To that loud faith for freedom (life more abundant)
Which we once professed shouting
Into the silent listening microphone
Or on an alien platform to a sea
Of white perplexed faces troubled
With secret Imperial guilt; shouting
Of you with a vision euphemistic
As you always appear
To your lonely sons on distant shores.

Then the cold sky and continent would disappear
In a grey mental mist.
And in its stead the hibiscus blooms in shameless scarlet
        and the bougainvillea in mauve passion
        entwines itself around strong branches;
        the palm trees stand like tall proud moral women
        shaking their plaited locks against the
        cool suggestive evening breeze;
        the short twilight passes;
        the white full moon turns its round gladness
        towards the swept open space
        between the trees; there will be
        dancing tonight; and in my brimming heart
        plenty of love and laughter.
        Oh, I got tired of the cold Northern sun

Of white anxious ghost-like faces
Of crouching over heatless fires
In my lonely bedroom.
The only thing I never tired of
Was the persistent kindness
Of you too few unafraid
Of my grave dusky strangeness.

So I came back
Sailing down the Guinea Coast.
Loving the sophistication
Of your brave new cities:
Dakar, Accra, Cotonou,
Lagos, Bathurst and Bissau;
Liberia, Freetown, Libreville,
Freedom is really in the mind.

Go up-country, so they said,
To see the real Africa.
For whomsoever you may be,
That is where you come from.
Go for bush, inside the bush,
You will find your hidden heart.
Your mute ancestral spirit.
And so I went, dancing on my way.

Now you lie before me passive
With your unanswering green challenge.
Is this all you are?
This long uneven red road, this occasional succession
Of huddled heaps of four mud walls
And thatched, falling grass roofs
Sometimes ennobled by a thin layer
Of white plaster, and covered with thin
Slanting corrugated zinc.
These patient faces on weather-beaten bodies

Bowing under heavy market loads.
The pedalling cyclist wavers by
On the wrong side of the road,
As if uncertain of this new emancipation.
The squawking chickens, the pregnant she-goats
Lumber awkwardly with fear across the road.
Across the windscreen view of my four-cylinder kit car
An overladen lorry speeds madly towards me
Full of produce, passengers, with driver leaning
Out into the swirling dust to pilot his
Swinging obsessed vehicle along.
Beside him on the raised seat his first-class
Passenger, clutching and timid; but he drives on
At so, so many miles per hour, peering out with
Bloodshot eyes, unshaved face and dedicated look;
His motto painted on each side: *Sunshine Transport,*
We get you there quick, quick. The Lord is my Shepherd.

The red dust settles down on the green leaves.

I know you will not make me want, Lord,
Though I have reddened your green pastures
It is only because I have wanted so much
That I have always been found wanting.
From South and East, and from my West
The sandy desert holds the North.
We look across a vast Continent
And blindly call it ours.
You are not a Country, Africa,
You are a concept,
Fashioned in our minds, each to each,
To hide our separate fears,
To dream our separate dreams.
Only those within you who know
Their circumscribed Plot,
And till it well with steady plough

Can from that harvest then look up
To the vast blue inside
Of the enamelled bowl of sky
Which covers you and say
"This is my Africa" meaning
"I am content and happy.
I am fulfilled, within,
Without and roundabout.
I have gained the little longings
Of my hands, my loins, my heart,
And the soul following in my shadow."
I know now that is what you are, Africa:
Happiness, contentment, and fulfilment,
And a small bird singing on a mango tree.

NYASALAND

James D. Rubadiri

STANLEY MEETS MUTESA

Such a time of it they had;
The heat of the day
The chill of the night
And the mosquitoes that followed.
Such was the time and
They bound for a kingdom.

The thin weary line of carriers
With tattered dirty rags to cover their backs;
The battered bulky chests
That kept on falling off their shaven heads.
Their tempers high and hot
The sun fierce and scorching
With it rose their spirits
With its fall their hopes
As each day sweated their bodies dry and
Flies clung in clumps on their sweat scented backs.
Such was the march
And the hot season just breaking.

Each day a weary pony dropped,
Left for the vultures on the plains;
Each afternoon a human skeleton collapsed,
Left for the Masai on the plains;
But the march trudged on
Its khaki leader in front
He the spirit that inspired.
He the light of hope.

Then came the afternoon of a hungry march,
A hot and hungry march it was;
The Nile and the Nyanza
Lay like two twins
Azure across the green countryside.
The march leapt on chaunting
Like young gazelles to a water hole.
Hearts beat faster
Loads felt lighter
As the cool water lapt their sore feet.
No more the dread of hungry hyenas
But only tales of valour when
At Mutesa's court fires are lit.
No more the burning heat of the day
But song, laughter and dance.

The village looks on behind banana groves,
Children peer behind reed fences.
Such was the welcome
No singing women to chaunt a welcome
Or drums to greet the white ambassador;
Only a few silent nods from aged faces
And one rumbling drum roll
To summon Mutesa's court to parley
For the country was not sure.

The gate of reeds is flung open,
There is silence
But only a moment's silence—
A silence of assessment.
The tall black king steps forward,
He towers over the thin bearded white man,
Then grabbing his lean white hand
Manages to whisper
"Mtu mweupe karibu"
White man you are welcome.
The gate of polished reed closes behind them
And the West is let in.

Marina Gashe

THE VILLAGE

Kanyariri, Village of Toil,
Village of unending work.
Like a never drying spring,
Old women dark and bent
Trudge along with their hoes
To plots of weedy maize.
Young wives like donkeys
From cock crow to setting of the sun
Go about their timeless duties,
Their scraggy figures like bows set in a row,
Plod up and down the rolling village farms
With loads on their backs
And babies tied to their bellies.
In the fields all day they toil
Stirring up the soil with hands and knives
Like chickens looking for worms.
Nothing here seems to sit still.
Even the village church is like a favourite well
Where the "Revivalists" with their loudspeakers
Never cease calling people
To confess their sins and drink the Water of Life.
At dawn men ride away leaving the womenfolk
To fend for the bony goats and the crying children.

GHANA

Kojo Gyinaye Kyei

THE TALKING DRUMS

I hear the beat
Of the drums,
The Atumpan drums,
Asante Kotpko:
Kum-apem-a-apem-beba!

I hear the beat
Of Prempeh drums,
Osei Tutu drums.

I hear the call
Of Nnawuta:
Tinn-tinn konn-konn!
Tinn-tinn konn-konn!
Konn-konn!

I ponder the valour
Of the mourned and mighty
African might.
I sense the resonance
Of Dawuro beats:
Tonn-tonn sann-sann!

Tonn-tonn sann-sann!
Sann-sann!

I muse upon Ghana,
Melle and Songhay.
I hear the echo
Of Fontomfrom,
The beat of
Mpintin drums:
Damirifa due . . . due!
Damirifi due . . . due!
Damirifi ooo-oo-o!

And *ooo!* The Sage!
Ankoanna Osagyefo
Bringing up the rear
At shoulders' acclaim:
The Sage who notched
Beauty and splendor
On Africa's glory!

I hear the beat
Of the drums!
I hear the beat
Of the Talking Drums!

AFRICAN IN LOUISIANA

I stopped deep
In Louisiana once,
A cop close at my heels:

What! Go to the colored side.
Don't sit here!

Somewhat angry,
But, indeed, hungry,
I could only say:
Some day we will meet again,
Your heart changed
For friendship.

I sat, though,
And was served soup
In a miracle-whip bottle
I still keep
For a keepsake.

Francis Ernest Kobina Parkes

THREE PHASES OF AFRICA

I MIDNIGHT

Lord 'tis midnight
Dark gloomy midnight
Midnight without stars.

Hush! it comes
And with it rise those ghosts
They rise the goblins with breath of flame
Midnight black and red of fire.

Mark, O mark the deep silence!

How can I not prefer
The noisy revolt

The push of life
To this which inspires naught but fear
Suggests naught but foul death.

The palm trees whisper rousing the sleeping vultures.

Lo the dogs are barking
They must have seen those ghosts
And beings with red hot breath
In this dark night.
Lord, what barking!

Silence again?
The witches have risen
And must have found a prey.
Alas for that sucking babe
Torn from its mother's breast
In this dark hour!
Mark its screams
Shrill,
Shriller yet,
Then . . .

That silence again!
They must have borne its pitious soul
Up, up the coconut tree
Where the vultures are waiting.

The wind blows.
Blows?
Sighs.
Sighs for the babe which blinded is.

Did you not hear a sound?
When?
Now. This jet black night

When ghosts have risen
And wicked gods wreck vengeance on the cursed.

Did you not hear that moan, that cry?
'Twas of that babe
Whose eyes have been gorged by those vultures vile
Those witches' stewards of the coconut tree.

That awe-inspiring silence once again.
And now I hear the tread of wicked gods.
I must not sleep, hag-ridden me
While those witches hack that hapless babe
Which blinded is
Up, up the tree.

See, see, my bed is wet
Wet with the sweat of my cold, cold frame
But I must not rise
At this dark gloomy hour
When the ghosts have risen
And the echoes are whistling
And the gods are all clanking
The chains on their feet.
No I must not rise
When the breath of flame
Makes this black night so red
And the witches are feeding
On the soul of that babe
Which the vultures have blinded.

Lord, still midnight?

II BLACKMAN'S GOD

Our God is great
Who dare deny it

Our God is great
Powerful and dark
Peering through ages
Healing, killing, guiding.

Our God is black
And like a goddamned god
Guiding when loving
Killing when angered.

Our God is powerful
All-powerful and black
And like all deities
Our Godhead likes blood
Whether it be blood of Isaac or ram
Our God likes blood.

Bloodthirsty and powerful is the blackman's God
And almighty, our God feeds lavish
Relishing all sacrifice
Preferring not
The thicketed ram
To childhood's innocent freedom.

Our God is like all gods
Hungering
For oblation
Thirsting
For the blood of Abel
And like all other gods
Our God must be the oppressor not the oppressed
Must point a cursing hand
And make us fugitives
And vagabonds tilling the unyielding vine.

Our God is immortal
Suffering's dread legacy
Affliction's living monument
Unchanged, unchanging, unchangeable.

Blackmen, heathens, idolaters,
Our God is like all gods
Slow to anger when fed fat on yams
And of great mercy when suckled on blood.

Brothers, blackmen, junglemen,
Our God is like all gods
Powerful and blood-loving
Go tell those priests
Messengers
Of gods across the seas
Since our God is powerful
And like their other gods
We will after no other
We stay here with our own
The graven image and the struggle
The hunted deer and libation
We stay here with the Eucharist
Of kpekple and palm nut soup.

III EVERY VALLEY SHALL BE EXALTED

Every valley shall upright stand
Earth's lowly ones shall rise
In black renascence

Let us burn bibles for incense
The rejected babe
Drowns in the man-made ravine
Storm-beaten, sun-scorched, fleeced

Out-dooring the star of the east?

They that ride
White asses
Shall roll in the debris of destruction
Their mind did fashion
Their banquet halls are doom
In ghosts awake
Their tabernacles of gold
Shall find their joyless grave.

Those that grope the sidewalks
Shall find resurrection
In crumbs of fulfilment

Those that chew oppression's bitter corn
Shall reap earth's joys
Their sweat did water
And mud huts rise
Above the rubbish heaps
Of yesteryear's cathedrals.

But them that from their hills of greed
Did scorn the toils of earth
Shall moan by empty gravesides
At the trumpet of awakening.

For the new dawn has broken
The upright palm goes to his farm
The mighty are no more
Cassocks are no more
Sceptres no more

The palm gives of its wine
At the sacramental font.

APOCALYPSE

In the last days,
Strange sights shall visit the earth.
Sights that may turn to blood the moon,
This sun to midnight—in the last days

But now, when swords are not yet ploughshares,
And spears still spears,
Hearken you, my little ones.

If walking, shaded by the mango tree,
Or running naked, scorched by this blazing sun,
You aught perceive
Now, while the arrow remains arrow,
And the miracle of spears and pruning hooks
Still remains an unseen miracle
Remember, my little ones
If perchance your infant feet do slide
And you find yourselves in some mysterious dungeon
Of black vengeful Sasabonsam,
In realms where dogs make speech,
And horns adorn the human front;
Where mermaids in their skirts of silvery scales
And chattering sea beasts flout mankind—
If in this strange sub-human realm
Your eyes fall on a stone, a hard black stone,
Lifeless and muddy, that has grown a beard,
Pray children, pass silently by.
Ask no questions.

For you are face to face with the first days
And the beginning and the end are one.

And in the end shall strange sights visit earth,
Stones shall be turned to men
And men to stones;
Sparrows beget eagles
And sand become good grain.

So children,
If perchance you see a hare that roars
Or an ape perched in a palanquin,
Look on in silence. Quickly pass by.
Quickly.

BLIND STEERSMEN

How can I, who cannot control
My own waking and dreaming, ever hope to make my voice heard
    in the wrangling for mankind's soul?

How can I, dumb in my own self-defence
Dream of forging words of salvation for billions
    with their cares and well-drugged silence?

Madness is virtue's beholding redemption in pools of blood
    squashed from dreams and inexpressible fears of men
    whose sole bastion is the booth
    (which also is the paschal knife)

Sanity lies in submitting to the bitter sweet dream
    created in factories of democracy by tired, drained-dry
    brains doped in senselessness by fact-effacing ether
    (which is their sole refuge)

And I, blown by thick puffs of factory smoke
    mad neither for my sorrows nor the world's,
    seek faith in the vision I know is false
    in sanity I know is mere soul-effacement

And my doubts catch up with me in the flitting cloud
    which cannot provide an anchor
    which is as empty as a dream
    and barren as the tomb

I, feeble, spineless speck, dare not hope by warm word, to
    wreck the sovereign peoples' dream
The salvation of the world lies in a deserted garden—
    in a blind worm's crawl.

F. K. Fiawoo

SOLILOQUY ON DEATH

The crows are come again to pick my eyes.
Oh, hard-hearted men of Anlo,
Come to my help.
But who dares come here?
I've no cowrie to give the ferryman—
And that is worse than death itself.
Oh, Kutsiami, how powerful are you,
Ferryman of all the spirits!
Rich and poor, kings and subjects of every rank—
All must come to you at last.
Away, foul crows!
Oh, ferryman, when I come to the water,
Ferry me across, asking no payment.
There is not a single soul in Anlo

Who would even give me a few cowries
To pay your toll.
Death, are you come
To lay hands upon your prey?

Ellis Ayitey Komey

OBLIVION

I want to remember the fallen palm
With whitening fluid of wine
Dripping from its hardened belly.
I want to remember it from the road
With mud on my feet
And thorn-scraped flesh
From the branches by the water.
I want to remember them well
The sight of the green eyed forest
The jubilant voices of the frogs
And the pleading cries of the owls.
I want to walk among the palms
With razor edged leaves
Shadowing the yam and the cassava scrubs
Under which the crab builds its castle
And the cocoa pods drooping like mothers'
Breasts feeding a hungry child.
I want to remember them all
Before they die and turn to mud
And I have gone.

THE DAMAGE YOU HAVE DONE

When I see blood pouring down the valleys,
Mahoganys trembling with fear
And palms drooping with disease,
I know you cannot stay with me
Nor hold a light across the land,
The damage you have done.

And when I remember how you looked
The first day you entered my hut,
A candle in one hand and a book in the other,
I know that your days are now gone
With the locust across the farm,
The damage you have done.

And when the first drop of rain
Manures the soil, now almost grey,
A hoe in one hand, wheat in the other
And a curse on the lips, I'll set to work
If the land is to recover
From the damage you have done.

Andrew Amankwa Opoku

RIVER AFRAM

Written in Twi, translated by the author

River, I am passing.
Red River whose head lies in the mountains,
I have pointed my face to the sea.
I am from Kwaforoamoa of old
Odomankoma-the-Creator's time.

I started not today,
I walk on the way still.
River, I am passing.

River, I am passing.
Red River that flows through red earth,
I go over stones,
I go over sand,
I have traversed a long way,
I have meandered and meandered,
Nothing can stop me.
River, I am passing.

River, I am passing.
I am passing at dawn.
By sunrise I shall be on the way.
Noon will bring travellers
To crowd my fords.
When the rowers plead with me
I shall not stop to help them pass.
River, I am passing.

River, I am passing.
I go over roots,
I go over the depths,
I bid it foam up before it foams.
If you dare me and measure with your foot
I shall make you slip and go before me.
A wayfarer companion is what I want.
River, I am passing.

River, I am passing.
I am passing with my children.
Set a basket trap
Or string in hooks,
Neither of these to me is foam.

There goes the Otidie fish,
The mudfish sallies forth.
River, I am passing.

River, I am passing.
I am overflowing your dams,
If it is for Odom and lobsters
That you dam me up,
You had better go home and rest;
Only the crab and the river snail
Deserve to be pitied.
River, I am passing.

River, I am passing.
Ogyamma fruits are ripe, calling upon farmers to mark out their farms.
New settlers have gone to start new farmsteads;
The palm-fronded shed on the bank calls me;
The monkey has espied from the treetops what is approaching.
The eagle has seen afar through the telescope
Civilization and inventions ushering in calamity, but
River, I am passing.

River, I am passing.
Let farm-goers pass on, too.
The forest is on yonder bank.
If you fear the crossing, your farm will be in the grassland;
I am diverting my tributaries and lagoons from you.
If you do not cross, you have nothing but roots;
You can drain my waters to catch the fish only when I dry up, but
River, I am passing.

River, I am passing.
Once my course was canopied
And my steps were timed to the flutter of the leaves;

Adum and mahogany and Abako
Cover my waters with shade
For the elephant, the buffalo and bush cow
To drink and regale themselves.
River, I am passing.

River, I am passing.
Today I go through wastes and arid savannah.
Thanks to Tete Quashie:
He has brought the tree of wealth and national upheaval
Into the country
And clans no longer group together,
But each individual scratches towards where money is.
River, I am passing.

River, I am passing.
I set out on the road a long while ago.
Daily I pass between rocks.
I am bearing all and sundry away.
The duiker that sleeps in the hollow of the buttress is afloat,
My flood waters have caught the orphan that floats on the wet log.
River, I am passing.

River, I am passing.
Those returning from farms will come to bathe
And the fisherfolk will dip nets for fish.
The benevolent one stops to receive thanks:
Praise knows its owner,
Therefore it never misses the way, it is never lost.
It will follow and overtake me, therefore
River, I am passing.

River, I am passing.
I am passing by yards;
When the wild pig ploughs right up to me,

With laughter I flow on;
No one engaged in battle with Osei tarries to feast on pork.
A year's journey we know
Begins with a single step.
River, I am passing.

River, I am passing.
I am passing how?
The leopard's watering place belongs to me,
The crocodile's lair is known to me,
The hatching place of the python
Is hidden near my bed,
I spoil the lizard's eggs.
River, I am passing.

River, I am passing.
I am carrying gold dust away,
I carry precious stones,
I lick silver, like pastilles.
I know the source of ore yet I dig no mine.
When you dive into me, prosperity,
Yet I am going into the sea to seek wealth.
River, I am passing.

River, I am passing.
Afram, the sacred river, I move fast.
Asiemire-the-Hunter says
He wants a chance to cross to the other side.
Odomankoma-the-Creator's Hunter,
First give me an egg because
No one goes to the plains without crossing me.
River, I am passing.

River, I am passing.
I bear a great tale.
Decisions of great moment taken yonder by the elders

Have been swept to me by the drain waters.
However wide I spread my floods,
So long as truth remains truth,
It will continue to float forever.
River, I am passing.

River, I am passing.
Before the hunting camp grew into a town
I was present,
When the town was going to become a state, I saw it.
When the elders were making the constitution I was passing this
way.
I am the very boundary between nations,
My testimony is beyond doubt.
River, I am passing.

River, I am passing.
I met the grandsires, I have seen the grandchildren.
This decaying past
In my presence would be repaired.
The unknown lies ahead of me yonder.
The day when Ataara set out to set the sea on fire
I bore him thither.
River, I am passing.

River, I am passing.
Ataara is preparing to go and fire the war-declaring shot.
He has made his bullets and ground his gunpowder.
He claims whatever belongs to the Kodiabe people.
When the hunter kills the buffalo
I don't partake of the meat,
When the buffalo kills the hunter, I don't go to his funeral, there-
fore
River, I am passing.

River, I am passing.
When Okoforoboo (Victor of the Heights) wins victory
He will cast off his ammunition bag to bathe in my waters;
When he suffers defeat he washes his tears in my waters;
If the battle fails to be staged,
He holds his drinking parties on my banks.
If they become annihilated I will show their ruins.
River, I am passing.

River, I am passing.
When Adu Bofoo was marshalling Osei's hosts to Krepi,
I ferried him across.
When he returned bringing the European captive
I gave him gifts of mudfish and drink of welcome.
If Christianity will reach Oseikurom (Kumase)
It was through my help that Ramseyer crossed over.
River, I am passing.

River, I am passing.
Buruku stands yonder clad in white cloth
And besmeared with white clay.
"Ant-never-climbs" has refused to accompany me.
He will not, he stands there for a cause.
High tower that was not built by any hand,
Rain-drenched stone,
It remains where it is, but as for me, I am.
River, I am passing.

River, I am passing.
I am going to make way for the generations that follow.
When adults live too long
Children become stunted;
If the present generation who drink my waters
Do not praise and extol me,
The latecomers who come to find clean water will speak.
River, I am passing.

River, I am passing.
Yet I listen to what goes on on the banks;
A grand play is in full swing there,
State drumming and horn-blowing continue in earnest.
The precentors have called me by my appellations,
The dancers have descended to invite me with their dance,
The damsels spin themselves like marbles upon the table.
River, I am passing.

River, I am passing.
Salute me with Atumpan drums.
I have risen in majesty.
Sound the gongs in my praise.
I who go forth
Am the same that returns.
River, I am passing.

River, I am passing.
I am going yonder to my origins.
When a trap releases it reverts to its original position.
The setting sun is ablaze behind the horizon.
In a few moments the moon will be up,
The pigeons and doves seek their nest,
The tired one has fed to repletion and is turning his pots.
River, I am passing.

River, I am passing.
In the same way man is passing, too.
Big river, I am passing and what of the rivulet?
The royal lord is passing and the servant is passing;
Nothing stops me and so nothing stops you, too.
When we come across the rock we flow over it,
During the dry season and the flood alike.
River, I am passing.

Kwesi Brew

A PLEA FOR MERCY

We have come to your shrine to worship—
We the sons of the land.
The naked cowherd has brought
The cows safely home,
And stands silent with his bamboo flute
Wiping the rain from his brow
As the birds brood in their nests
Awaiting the dawn with unsung melodies;
The shadows crowd on the shores
Pressing their lips against the bosom of the sea;
The peasants home from their labours
Sit by their log-fires
Telling tales of long ago.
Why should we, the sons of the land,
Plead unheeded before your shrine
When our hearts are full of song
And our lips tremble with sadness?
The little firefly vies with the star,
The log-fire with the sun
The water in the calabash
With the mighty Volta,
But we have come in tattered penury
Begging at the door of a Master.

THE SEARCH

The past
Is but the cinders

Of the present;
The future
The smoke
That escaped
Into the cloud-bound sky.

Be gentle, be kind, my beloved,
For words become memories,
And memories tools
In the hands of jesters.
When wise men become silent,
It is because they have read
The palms of Christ
In the face of the Buddha.

So look not for wisdom
And guidance
In their speech, my beloved.
Let the same fire
Which chastened their tongues
Into silence,
Teach us—teach us!

The rain came down,
When you and I slept away
The night's burden of our passions;
Their new-found wisdom
In quick lightning flashes
Revealed the truth
That they had been
The slaves of fools.

THE LONELY TRAVELLER

Leave him alone, sweet enemy,
For the mothers of the earth
Have sanctioned his freedom;
And in priceless peace
He floats in ethereal bliss,
A traveller on the shores of eternity.
You saw the genial mists of courage:
With his faith as his spear
And his past as his shield,
He battled the bondage of bludgeons
Now far on the horizon
The red suns set,
The tired suns set
To turn old nights into new dawns,
And people the skies with black stars.
And our hands that slept on the drums
Have found their cunning
To cheer the lonely traveller
Meandering his weary way
On the green and golden hills of Africa.

ANCESTRAL FACES

They sneaked into the limbo of time,
But could not muffle the gay jingling
Bells on the frothy necks
Of the sacrificial sheep
That limped and nodded after them:
They could not hide the moss on the pate

Of their reverent heads,
And the gnarled bark of the wawa trees,
Nor the rust on the ancient state-swords,
Nor the skulls studded with grinning cowries.
They could not silence the drums,
The fibre of their souls and ours—
The drums that whisper to us
Behind black sinewy hands.
They gazed and
Sweeping like white locusts through the forests
Saw the same men, slightly wizened,
Shuffle their sandalled feet to the same rhythms.
They heard the same words of wisdom uttered
Between puffs of pale blue smoke.
They saw us and said:
They have not changed!

K. B. Jones-Quartey

STRANGER, WHY DO YOU WONDER SO?

Is it the fecundating life you see around
That makes you wonder so,
O Stranger to our land?

Is it the impenetrable mass
Of tree and shrub and vine,
So vapour-hung and brooding,
So sparked with mystic sound
And yet so still, so still
With an innumerable silence?

Is it the countless fluttering
Of the feathered wing;
The hum and drone of bugs
Intent upon their eternal chore
Of torture and of death to man?
The terror of unseen beasts,
The marrow-chilling cry of the small tree-bear
That drives the stranger out of his mind?

Is it the ugly vulture hovering low
Over the teeming dung upon the heap;
The croaking frog,
The viperous snake,
The army of voracious ants,
The million lizards in the sun?

Is it the sightless beggar
Moaning on the ground,
The noisesome children turned adrift,
The market bursting with disordered life?

Is it the naked, naked babe
Positioned to a naked back,
Positioned to receive the milk
Free-flowing from a naked breast?

Is it such things that make you wonder so?

Take heart, O stranger to our land.
Tomorrow, we shall have the forest cleared,
The vulture will espy no dung,
The child and mother will be clothed,
The snake will turn its poison on itself,
The small tree-bear look down
From museum walls, without a cry.

Give us but the morrow:
Make way for Africa
In the march to heaven—
Or to hell.

And would that make you wonder less,
O Stranger to our land?

Michael Dei-Anang

MY AFRICA

I love the days of long ago,
Great days of virtuous chastity
When wild men and wilder beasts
Kept close company.

I love Africa as herself—
Unsophisticated queenly Africa,
That precious pearl of the past.
Not all her beauties were the best
Nor all her charms the highest
In the days of long ago.

But give me back that Africa,
With all her best and all her worst,
Then leave me free to plan anew
Great God's own Africa,
Charged with the charms of long ago.
Yet give me, too, from far away lands
The fertile laws of Faraday.

Give me these,
And out of that long-lost Africa

Will rise, phoenix-like,
A New-World Africa.

When vision was short
And knowledge scant,
Men called me *Dark Africa*

Dark Africa?
I, who raised the regal pyramids
And held the fortunes
Of Conquering Caesars
In my tempting grasp.

Dark Africa?
Who nursed the doubtful child
Of civilization
On the wand'ring banks
Of the life-giving Nile,
And gave to the teeming nations
Of the West a Grecian gift.

The dazzling glare of iron and steel
Sometimes obscures non-metal's worth,
So when I held close
My pristine bows and arrows,
And cared not much for iron and steel
Men called me *Dark*.
But dearer far than steel and iron
Is the tranquil art
Of thinking together
And living together.

I know a world,
A trampled world,
Partitioned and pawned
In centuries of greed

And still undone—
My Africa.

A waking world,
Rising now
From age-long slumber,
Fresh with the strength
That follows rest—
My Africa.

I love a world,
This priceless world,
Sweet home of haunting melodies
And roll of tom-toms—
My Africa.

I'll die for a world,
A wonderful world,
No other land
Nor East nor West
Attracts me so—
My Africa.

Aquah Laluah

SHADOW OF DARKNESS

Shadow of Darkness, listen I am calling.
Night comes upon us, heavy dew is falling.
You are powerful as the night!

Your breath is sweet as the earth.
Your eye more gentle than a woman's.
Your horn, the curved bows of two moons.

On your forehead is the star of morning,
On your back the eagle;
Under your tongue the hump of a beetle,
Beautiful bull from the line of Osiris.

Your feet are beautiful in strength
Your voice is deep as the thunder.

Listen I am calling, calling, calling.
Oh, I need you; I am lonely.
Come to me quickly—Shadow of Darkness.

NATIVITY

Within a native hut, ere stirred the dawn,
Unto the Pure One was an Infant born,
Wrapped in blue lappah that His mother dyed,
Laid on His father's home-tanned deerskin hide,
The Babe still slept, by all things glorified.
Spirits of black bards burst their bonds and sang
"Peace upon earth" until the heavens rang.
All the black babies who from earth had fled
Peeped through the clouds—then gathered round His head,
Telling of things a baby needs to do,
When first he opes his eyes on wonder new;
Telling Him that sleep was sweetest rest,
All comfort came from His black mother's breast.
Their gift was Love, caught from the springing sod,
Whilst tears and laughter were the gifts of God.
Then all the Wise Men of the past stood forth,
Filling the air, East, West, and South and North,
And told Him of the joy that wisdom brings
To mortals in their earthly wanderings.

The children of the past shook down each bough,
Wreathed frangipani blossoms for His brow,
They put pink lilies in His mother's hand,
And heaped for both the first fruits of the land.
His father cut some palm fronds, that the air
Be coaxed to zephyrs while He rested there.
Birds trilled their hallelujahs; all the dew
Trembled with laughter, till the Babe laughed too.
Black women brought their love so wise,
And kissed their motherhood into His mother's eyes.

G. Adali-Mortti

PALM LEAVES OF CHILDHOOD

When I was very small indeed,
and Joe and Fred were six-year giants,
my father, they and I, with soil
did mix farm-yard manure.
In this we planted coconuts,
naming them by brothers' names.
The palms grew faster far than I;
and soon, ere I could grow a Man,
they, flowering, reached their goal!
Like the ear-rings that my sisters wore
came the tender golden flowers.
I watched them grow from gold to green;
then nuts as large as Tata's head.
I craved the milk I knew they bore.
I listened to the whispering leaves:
to the chattering, rattling, whispering leaves,
when night winds did wake.
They haunt me still in work and play:

those whispering leaves behind the slit
on the cabin wall of childhood's
dreaming and becoming.

A. L. Milner-Brown

WHO KNOWS?

Who knows? This Africa so richly blest
With golden lands and fronded palms in air,
The envy of great nations far and near,
May yet the world lead back to peace and rest,
Goodwill to all. Who knows? Who knows?

And when the fullness of God's time has come
And men of divers colors, tribes and castes
Have owned Him King; when hate and sin are passed,
The Prince of Peace may found His home
In Africa at last. Who knows? Who knows?

Edwin Barclay

HUMAN GREATNESS

The starry hosts whose far-flung cohorts gleam
With silvery radiance on the Capes of Night
Have quenched their bivouac-fires and in wild flight
Are hastening like a panic haunted stream
Of crushed battalions. Mighty did they seem—
The flaming bulwarks of eternity—
But now, for all their glorious pageantry,
The filmy remnant of a faded dream.
O History! Upon thy glowing page
Time writes her judgments, but she writes in vain;
Her symbols man misreads in every age,
And garners thence but legacies of pain.
Then why lift up, O man, your heart in pride?
You are but dust and even Caesar died.

Roland Tombekai Dempster

IS THIS AFRICA?

Is this Africa
unfair men once called

Continent of Darkness
land of baboons, apes and monkeys,
cannibals and men with tails
only fit to be
the servants of other men?

Is this the same Africa
now holding firm her own,
deciding her own fate,
with the sword of faith
fighting her foes
with weapons holier than those
used by the "master-race"?

Is this Africa
in dignity and grace
nowhere surpassed,
in wisdom deep?

Can this be the same Africa,
now center of hope,
of which men once spoke
in vilest terms?

Is this Africa,
Mother Africa,
long suppressed, divided,
ruled, impugned?
How proud are we today, Africa,
to note the part you play
for your sons and daughters
still washed in tears.

AFRICA'S PLEA

I am not you—
but you will not
give me a chance,
will not let me be *me*.

"If I were you"—
but you know
I am not you,
yet you will not
let me be *me*.

You meddle, interfere
in my affairs
as if they were yours
and you were me.

You are unfair, unwise,
foolish to think
that I can be you,
talk, act
and think like you.

God made me *me*.
He made you *you*.
For God's sake
Let me be *me*.

Gabriel Okara

PIANO AND DRUMS

When at break of day at a riverside
I hear jungle drums telegraphing
the mystic rhythm, urgent, raw
like bleeding flesh, speaking of
primal youth and the beginning,
I see the panther ready to pounce,
the leopard snarling about to leap
and the hunters crouch with spears poised;

And my blood ripples, turns torrent,
topples the years and at once I'm
in my mother's lap a suckling;
at once I'm walking simple
paths with no innovations,
rugged, fashioned with the naked
warmth of hurrying feet and groping hearts
in green leaves and wild flowers pulsing.

Then I hear a wailing piano
solo speaking of complex ways
in tear-furrowed concerto;
of faraway lands
and new horizons with

coaxing diminuendo, counterpoint,
crescendo. But lost in the labyrinth
of its complexities, it ends in the middle
of a phrase at a daggerpoint.

And I, lost in the morning mist
of an age at a riverside, keep
wandering in the mystic rhythm
of jungle drums and the concerto.

YOU LAUGHED AND LAUGHED AND LAUGHED

In your ears my song
is motor car misfiring
stopping with a choking cough;
and you laughed and laughed and laughed.

In your eyes my ante-
natal walk was inhuman passing
your "omnivorous understanding"
and you laughed and laughed and laughed.

You laughed at my song
You laughed at my walk.

Then I danced my magic dance
to the rhythm of talking-
drums pleading, but you shut your
eyes and laughed and laughed and laughed.

And then I opened my mystic
inside wide like

the sky, instead you entered your
car and laughed and laughed and laughed.

You laughed at my dance
you laughed at my inside.

You laughed and laughed and laughed.
But your laughter was ice-block
laughter and it froze your inside froze
your voice froze your ears
froze your eyes and froze your tongue.

And now it's my turn to laugh;
but my laughter is not ice-block
ice-block laughter. For I
know not cars, know not ice-blocks.

My laughter is the fire
of the eye of the sky, the fire
of the earth, the fire of the air
the fire of the seas and the
rivers fishes animals trees
and it thawed your inside,
thawed your voice, thawed your
ears, thawed your eyes, and
thawed your tongue.

So a meek wonder held
your shadow and you whispered:
"Why so?"
And I answered:
"Because my fathers and I
are owned by the living
warmth of the earth
through our naked feet."

WERE I TO CHOOSE

When Adam broke the stone
And red streams raged down to
Gather in the womb
An angel calmed the storm;

And I, the breath mewed
In Cain, unblinking gaze
At the world without
From the brink of an age

That draws from the groping lips
A breast-muted cry
To thread the years.
(O were I to choose).

And now the close of one
And thirty turns, the world
Of bones is Babel, and
The different tongues within
Are flames the head
Continually burning.

And O of this dark halo
Were the tired head free.

And when the harmattan
Of days has parched the throat
And skin, and sucked the fever
Of the head away,

Then the massive dark
Descends, and flesh and bone

Are razed. And (O were I
To choose) I'd cheat the worms
And silence seek in stone.

THE CALL OF THE RIVER NUN

I hear you call
I hear it far away
I hear it break the circle
Of these crouching hills.

I hear your call
I want to view your face
Again and feel your cold
Embrace or at your brim
To set myself
And inhale your breath
Or like the trees to watch
My mirrored self unfold
And span my days
With song from the lips of dawn.

I hear your call
I hear it coming through
Invoking the ghost of a child
Listening where river-birds hail
Your silver surfaced flow.

I hear your call
My river's calling too
Its ceaseless flow impels
My foundering canoe down
Its inevitable course.

And each dying
Year brings near the sea-birds
Call the final call
That stills the crested waves
And breaks in two the curtain
Of silence of my upturned canoe.

O inevitable God
Shall my pilot be
My inborn stars to that
Final call to Thee?
O my river's complex course.

ONCE UPON A TIME

Once upon a time, son
they used to laugh with their hearts
and laugh with their eyes;
but now they only laugh with their teeth,
while their ice-block-cold eyes
search behind my shadow.

There was a time indeed
they used to shake hands with their hearts;
but that's gone, son.
Now they shake hands without hearts
while their left hands search
my empty pockets.

"Feel at home," "Come again,"
they say, and when I come
again and feel
at home, once, twice,

there will be no thrice—
for then I find doors shut on me.

So I have learned many things, son.
I have learned to wear many faces
like dresses—homeface,
officeface, streetface, hostface, cock-
tailface, with all their conforming smiles
like a fixed portrait smile.

And I have learned too
to laugh with only my teeth
and shake hands without my heart.
I have also learned to say, "Goodbye,"
when I mean "Goodriddance";
to say "Glad to meet you,"
without being glad; and to say "It's been
nice talking to you," after being bored.

But believe me, son.
I want to be what I used to be
when I was like you. I want
to unlearn all these muting things.
Most of all, I want to relearn
how to laugh, for my laugh in the mirror
shows only my teeth like a snake's bare fangs!

So show me, son,
how to laugh; show me how
I used to laugh and smile
once upon a time when I was like you.

TO ADHIAMBO

I hear many voices
like it's said a madman hears;
I hear trees talking
like it's said a medicine man hears.

Maybe I'm a madman,
I'm a medicine man.

Maybe I'm mad;
for the voices are luring me,
urging me from the midnight
moon and the silence of my desk
to walk on wave crests across a sea.

Maybe I'm a medicine man
hearing talking saps,
seeing behind trees;
but who's lost his powers
of invocation.

But the voices and the trees
are one name spelling and one figure
silence-etched across
the moonface is walking, stepping
over continents and seas.

And I raised my hand—
my trembling hand, gripping
my heart as handkerchief
and waved and waved—and waved—
but she turned her eyes away.

Francesca Yetunde Pereira

THE PARADOX

The cross, the icon
The disciples fought
They are still fighting
The whiteman claims
His god supreme
And blackman muses
White god, in reason can I hope for grace bestowed,
The disciples fought. They are still fighting, maybe
Somewhere in white clouds, somewhere in blackest
Abyss, the white god and the black god dumb,
Look silently on.
The disciples fought
They all of them join
Battle, fierce raging,
Each god is mighty.
They must be. It must be. The world is constant in its chaos.
The world is crumbling and all gods are silent. Evil begets
Good begets evil. Watching. Wenching Eves, empty headed apes
Demanding, exacting. Their folly drowning in spirits flowing.
And the Infant, crying
For the dried-up stream
The lapped-up stream
Caked stream of life
Is milked in a manger
Sawdust and straw.
Cool breeze fleeting
Past suspense, hope,
And prophecy. Empty.
The age old tree without, magnificent, proudly stands
Its yellowing leaves waft to and fro against the deep

Blue sky. The mind persists in calmness, and frenzy
Beats a wild resounding drum within the tortured heart.
Learn patience
O frenzied drumbeat
Be still and rein
Thyself. Advent of
Destiny. Wildly yours.
Then canst thou beat
Wild wild refrain
And drum and dance
For joy. Or rend
Dumb heavens with
Thy woes. The age
Old tree, the cheery
Room, the bright blue
Sky above. The drum
Still blind, beats on.
The fevered drum still blind beats wildly fiercely on.
No crumbs fall from the orgies of the rich. Eves and apes
With licentious smell trampling the earth.
Under their feet the bones of infants. Disciples still
Fighting. Each god is mighty. The world is crumbling. And gods are silent.

MOTHER DARK

Mother Land
Long lain asleep
Her people loved
They lived
And killed to live
By Nature's law.

Souls to save
The strangers sought,
Riches, some knowledge,
They named her "Dark"
Yes, dark was she
In every sense was dark.

They brought "The Light"
And with the light
She saw her children
Led in chains
Their wearied steps
Quickened by
The lash of Cain.

The light-bearers
Hooded with repentance
Philanthropy
With glib tongue
Took the land
Claimed rulers
With gifts of tinsel
Paltry gifts
With crumbs they fed
The children of dark.
The bearers of the light
Ate succulent steak.

Mother Dark
She was dark, very dark
Cried out
And her voice shook all the world,
Free my people
Set my sons and daughters
Free!

The bearers of light
Made bold retreat
Silent dignified farewell
Pomp and splendour, saving grace
The spoilt child
Amidst a thousand shells
Withdrew.

Mother Dark
Her rulers chose
All branded with her mark.
Alas! They learned too well the "light"
Then brought home the yoke.

Mother Dark
Her wounded heart
Wailed loud in pain,
Is there no hope?
My children perish!
But her voice is not heard
For her children now
Oppress her children.

THE BURDEN

Tell me no secret, friend,
My heart will not sustain
Its load, too heavily
On my mind to weigh.

Involve me not, friend,
Make not of me a mute.
Like a labyrinth

The road from my heart
Winds round and round,
Yet leads to an avenue—
The boulevard of speech.

Tell me no secret, friend,
To you I'll still be true.
For you I'll fight
No matter where—
But make not a mute of me.

TWO STRANGE WORLDS

Women,
What fools we are,
Invading unprotected
The world of men so alien,
And ever manifesting
Weakness in tenderness.

In that world of reason,
Is it not reason to give?
Willing converts
Ardent learners
Giving, giving.

But, fools—
Our hearts have lost
The room for reason.
Can we unlearn
That which was taught?

Can we survive?
How can we live?
The flame is out,
The cinders
Painful memories.

Frank Aig-Imoukhuede

ONE WIFE FOR ONE MAN

Italicized line-by-line translation from West African pidgin-English by Francis Ernest Kobina Parkes

I done try go to church, I done go for court.
I've tried the altar, I've tried the court-room.
Dem all dey talk about di *new culture*
All both of them talk about is this "new culture."
Dem talk about *equality*, dem mention *divorce.*
They talk about "equality" and proclaim "divorce."
Dem holler am so-tay my ear nearly cut;
They shout it so much my ear-drums nearly burst:
One wife for one man.

My fader before my fader get him wife barku.
My father's father had plenty of wives.
E no' get equality palaver; he live well
He did all right without all this "equality" humbug.
For he be oga for im own house.
And he was the boss in his own house.
Bot dat time done pass before white man come wit im
But since then the white man's come with this stuff about
One wife for one man.

Tell me how una woman no go make *yonga*
Tell me how a man can keep a woman from being bossy
Wen'e know say na 'im only dey.
When she knows well she has no lawful rival.
Suppose say-make God no 'gree-'e no born at all.
Suppose it is God's will she has no offspring at all.
A' tell you dat man bind dey craze wey start
I tell you the man must've been crazy who suggested
One wife for one man.

Jus' tell me how one wife fir do one man?
Just tell me how one wife can be enough for a man?
How man go fit stay all time for him house,
What can make a man stay home all the time
For when belle done kommotu.
When his one wife is pregnant as she can be?
How many pickin, self, one woman fir born
After all, how many children can one woman bear
When there's just one wife for one man?

Suppose self, say na so-so woman your wife dey born;
Suppose your wife's womb houses only females;
Suppose your wife sabe book, no' sabe make chop;
Suppose your wife is educated and doesn't know how to cook;
Den, how you go tell man make 'e no go out
Then how can you tell a man not to run around—
Sake of dis divorce? Bo, dis culture no waya o!
Or he'll be threatened by divorce. Man, this "new culture"
is awful:
Just one wife for one man!

John Pepper Clark

AGBOR DANCER

See her caught in the throb of a drum
Tippling from hide-brimmed stem
Down lineal veins to ancestral core,
Opening out in her supple tan limbs
Like fresh foliage in the sun.

See how entangled in the magic maze of music
In trance she treads the intricate pattern,
Rippling crest after crest to meet
The green clouds of the forest.

Tremulous beats wake trenchant
In heart a descant
Tingling quick to her finger tips
And toes virginal habits long
Too atrophied for pen or tongue.

Could I, early sequestered from my tribe,
Free a lead-tethered scribe,
I would answer her communal call,
Lose myself in her warm caress
Intervolving earth, sky and flesh.

FULANI CATTLE

The beef for Lagos is driven hundreds
of miles from the North on the hoof

Contrition twines me like a snake
Each time I come upon the wake

Of your clan undulating on the road in agony,
Your face the stool of mystery.
What secret hope or knowledge,
Locked in your hump away from man,
Imbues you with courage
So mute, so fiercely won
That, not demurring or kicking,
You go to the house of slaughter?
Can it be in the forging
Of your gnarled and crooked horn
You experience passions far stronger
Than storms which brim the Niger?
Perhaps the driver's whip no more
On your balding hind and crest
Arouses shocks of ecstasy.
Or likely the drunken journey
From desert through grass and forest
To the hungry town by the sea
Does call for rest.
But will you not first vouchsafe me—
Since the long knife must prevail—
The patience of your tail?

Christopher Okigbo

LAMENT OF THE FLUTES

with two flutes

TIDEWASH . . . Memories
fold-over-fold free-furrow,
mingling old tunes with new.
Tidewash . . . Ride me
memories, astride on firm
saddle, wreathed with white
lilies and roses of blood . . .

Sing to the rustic flute:
Sing a new note . . .

Where are the Maytime flowers,
where the roses? What will the
Watermaid bring at sundown,
a garland? A handful of tears?

Sing to the rustic flute:
Sing a new note . . .

Comes Dawn
gasping thro worn lungs,
Day breathes,
panting like torn horse—

We follow the wind to the fields
Bruising grass leafblade and corn . . .

Sundown: I draw in my egg head.
Night falls
smearing sore bruises with *Sloan's*,
boring new holes in old sheets—

We hear them, the talkative pines,
And nightbirds and woodnymphs afar off . . .

Shall I answer their call,
Creep on my underself
out of my snug hole, out of my shell
to the rocks and the fringe for cleansing?
Shall I offer to *Idoto*
my sandhouse and bones,
then write no more on snow patch?

Sing to the rustic flute:
Sing a new note.

Chuba Nweke

MOON SONG

Gather, ye brave sons of Ukadi Awaka!
I bring you my moon song
To sing on moonlit sands at night.
Oh, great musicians of Ukadi Awaka,
Your silver bands and flutes of gold
That brought smiles and tears alike
Will no more rock the town.

When we were young and lived for joy
A thing of beauty it used to be—
Emeka, his flute oiled to soar and sing,
Would steal the secret of each heart's desire
And make it public.

Gone are those sweet days
Of love and joy
When we laughed aloud—
Even in time of need.

Gather, ye brave ones of Ukadi Awaka!
I bring you my moon song
To sing on moonlit sands at night
In joy or sorrow alike.

Dennis C. Osadebay

THE AFRICAN TRADER'S COMPLAINT

I was a humble clerk,
They told me I was stupid

And that my laziness
Made me prefer to sit
All day and push a pen;
I bore the insult bravely
And planned to break the chain
That tied me to the table.

I broke the chain one day
And took to petty trading;
Fair Fortune smiled on me
And my business expanded;
I tried my hand at imports
But monopolies frowned;
I then exported produce,
Once more they played me down.

Big Business never loves—
Like tyrant western ranchers—
The bold determined nester;
You must become their clerk
Or buy your goods from them;
This is the burden I bear.
Would you insist I'm lazy
Because I am an African?

Adebayo Faleti

INDEPENDENCE

Translated from the Yoruba by Bakare Gbadamosi and Ulli Beier

There is nothing as sweet as independence.
It is a great day on which the slave buys his freedom.
When a slave can go to fetch water

And nobody can tell him: you are coming late!
When a slave will fetch firewood
And use it to cook his own food!
When a slave can bring home a couple of yams
Everyday, to use for his meal.
When the slave does not serve anybody,
When he is merely serving himself!
What a day, when the slave wakes up to rest—
Not to go to another man's farm!
When the slave starts planting his own farm.
Four hundred and twenty rows of yam!
When he will plant the maize and dig the yam.
When he will sell his crop and use it for his own family.
No longer will he do unpaid work.
No longer waste his old age serving others.
The slave will rejoice, rejoice, rejoice.
He will jump up into the air and slap his body with his arms.
He will sing the song and say:
"Help me to be thankful I am lucky!"
Let us rejoice with the slave.
The one whose life has never been pawned
Does not know the hardship of work before dawn.
A person who has never been a slave
Does not know the hardship of the stable boy.
He will never know what it means
To brush the dew off the leaves in the morning
And stay on the farm until after dark—slicing yams.
In the dry season or in the rainy season—
There is no escape from it.
The eyes of the slave have seen many things.
If a man's life is pawned
And he is as tall as the Ogun tree in the king's market,
He is as small as a dwarf terrier in the eyes of his master.
And if the master is burnt out like an old stick,
And if he is mangy like a scruffy old dog,
He will still be acting like the master.

The eyes of the slave have seen everything!
No day is like the day when the elephant served under the duiker.
Duiker sent elephant to the river,
But elephant did not return in time.
Duiker beat elephant.
Duiker abused elephant on the bridge.
He reminded elephant that he was rich enough to own him.
But the elephant accepted the punishment with love.
He said: it is not because I am stupid,
Or because I have not grown up.
If the slave moves carefully,
He may still buy his freedom after a long, long time.
It was not too late for the elephant
To buy himself free and become the head of the animals.
Let us learn wisdom from the elephant.
Let us shake off our suffering with patience.
Gently we kill the fly on our own body.
Let all of us get ready to buy ourselves back!
After all: we have land, and we have hoes.
We have cocoa trees and we have bananas.
We have palm kernels and we have groundnuts.
Let us fight, so that we may cultivate our own farm.
To escape from being slaves and pawns,
Let all our people be free.

Wole Soyinka

ABIKU

> Abiku *is the Yoruba myth of infant mortality, meaning literally, "born-to-die." It is believed that the dead child returns to plague the mother*

In vain your bangles cast
Charmed circles at my feet.

I am Abiku, calling for the first
And repeated time.

Must I weep for goats and cowries,
For palm oil and the sprinkled ash?
Yams do not sprout in armlets
To earth Abiku's limbs.

So when the snail is burnt in his shell
With the heated fragment, brand me
Deeply on the breast. You must know him
When Abiku calls again.

I am the squirrel teeth, cracked.
The riddle of the palm. Remember
This and dig me deeper still into
The god's swollen foot.

Once and the repeated time
Ageless though I puke. And when
You pour libations, each finger
Points me near the way I came, where

The ground is wet with mourning,
White dew suckles flesh-birds,
Evening befriends the spider,
Trapping flies in wine-froth.

Night, and Abiku sucks the oil
From lamps. Mothers! I'll be the
Suppliant snake coiled on the doorstep,
Yours the killing cry.

The ripest fruit was saddest.
Where I crept, the warmth was cloying.
In the silence of webs Abiku moans
Shaping mounds from the yolk.

Peter Clarke

PLAY SONG

Let's go up to the hillside today
    to play, to play
    to play.

Up to the hill where the daisies grow
    like snow, like snow
    like snow.

There shall we make a daisy chain
One tomorrow and tomorrow again
There where the daisies grow like snow
There's where we will go.

Let us go down to the little bay
    to play, to play
    to play.

Down to the bay where the children swim
    like fish, like fish
    like fish.

Down to the bay where the children swim,
Down to the bay where the white yachts skim,

Or up to the hill where the daisies grow,
There's where we will go.

IN AIR

Five gleaming crows
Are
Big, black forms

Five black crows
Are
Creatures floating

Five black creatures
Floating
On wide-stretched air

Five gleaming forms
Are
Blackly floating

Five gleaming crows
Float blackly
On wide-stretched air.

YOUNG SHEPHERD BATHING HIS FEET

Only the short, broad, splayed feet
Moved . . .

Feet that had trodden over
Soft soil,
Sand,
Ploughed veld,
Mountain rocks
And along narrow tracks,
On Winter clay and
Dust of
Summer roads . . .

The short, broad, splayed feet
Moved
In and out . . .

The stumpy toes stretched wide
Apart
And closed together
Then opened wide . . .

In ecstasy.

Bloke Modisane

ONE THOUGHT FOR MY LADY

One thought into one word,
One single vision of a word,
Like a thought, diffused
In the forever silence:
The opium-cure of make-believe.

One jester masks heart pangs,
Another the blood,

Nakedness, the other:
Drunkenness the lot,
In the ribald rigmarole
Revel of reverberations.

One fool's cape,
Dazzling patterns of color:
Red, yellow;
Weave a coward's pledge,
A brave man's badge.
All is drunkenness;
Not all is falsehood.
Just one side of the cape is real.

Which?

The cape jokes about the truth:
Parallel images of color, not meaning;
Private asides,
Too personal for sound.
The vision absolute,
The diversion of hollow sounds;
To stray truth into a thought
Around a vision
Always without words.

blue black

God!
glad I'm black;
pitch-forking devil black:
black, black, black;
black absolute of life complete,

greedfully grabbing life's living,
stupor drunkenness,
happiness.
depth of hurt,
anger of sorrow:
synthesis of joy, sadness;
composite child of life.
pulsating,
brash;
hatred coarse,
joy smooth.
stupid,
solomon wise;
sallow,
coconut-tree tall.
confused,
sure.
diverse continent:
cape mild,
acrid scorching sahara,
temperate mediterranean.
sun-total black;
the one that is I,
the one, no-one,
that is us all.

black blues

the blues is the black o' the face,
I said: black is the blues' face;
it's black in the mornin'
beige in the sun,
and blue black all night long.

Oh, the blues is a black devil face,
I said: devil black is the blues' face;
it's black in the mornin'
beige in the sun,
and blue black all night long.

my baby, said to me, daddy;
sit down and listen, candy:
the blues is in your blood,
black down deep in your skin
and the devil rides on your back.
The mean black blues got my daddy,
those black mean blues got you, daddy;
you're black in the mornin'
beige in the sun,
candy black all night long.

LONELY

it gets awful lonely,
lonely;
like screaming,
screaming lonely;
screaming down dream alley,
screaming blues, like none can hear;
but you hear clear and loud:
echoing loud;
like it's for you.
I talk to myself when I write,
shout, scream to myself;
then back to myself
scream and shout,
shouting a prayer,
screaming noises,

knowing this way I tell
the world about what still lives;
even maybe
just to scream and shout.
is it I lack the musician's contact
direct?
the smell of human bodies;
or, is it true, the writer
creates
(except the trinity with God,
the machine and He)
incestuous silhouettes
to each other scream and shout,
to me shout and scream
pray and mate;
inbred deformities of loneliness?

A. C. Jordan

YOU TELL ME TO SIT QUIET

Originally written in Xhosa. Translated into English by the author himself

You tell me to sit quiet when robbed of my manhood,
With nowhere to live and nought to call my own,
Now coming, now going, wandering and wanting,
No life in my home save the drone of the beetle!
    Go tell the worker bees,
    True guards of the hive,
    Not to sting the rash hunter
    Who grabs at their combs.

You tell me to sit quiet when robbed of my children,
All offered as spoils to the rich of the land,

To be hungered of body, retarded of mind,
And drained of all spirit of freedom and worth!
        Go tell the mother hen
        Who sits on her brood
        Not to peck at the mongrel
        That sniffs at her young.

You tell me, a poor mother widowed so young,
Bereft of my husband by mine-dust disease,
To let my poor orphans be ravaged by hunger,
For fear of the gendarmes and swart pick-up vans!
        Go tell the mother dove
        Who loves her fledglings
        Not to dare the fleet falcons
        While seeking for food.

You tell me, in spite of the light I've espied—
The light, the one legacy true and abiding—
To let my own kindred remain in the darkness,
Not knowing the glories of learning and living!
        Go tell the proud roosters
        That perch on the trees
        Not to sing loud their praises
        To sunrise at dawn.

You tell me, in spite of the riches of knowledge
Unveiled all around, replenishing the earth,
To live here forever enslaved by the darkness
Of ignorance, abject, and empty of mind!
        Go tell the drooping grass,
        Frost-bitten and pale,
        Not to quicken when roused
        By the warm summer rains.

Tell the winter not to give birth to spring.
Tell the spring not to flower into summer.

Tell the summer not to mellow into autumn.
Tell the morning-star not to herald the day.
Tell the darkness
Never to flee
When smitten at dawn
By the shafts of the sun.

Peter Abrahams

ME, COLORED

an extract from Tell Freedom

Aunt Liza.
Yes?
What am I?
What are you talking about?
I met a boy at the river.
He said he was Zulu.
She laughed.
You are Colored.
There are three kinds of people:
White people, Colored people,
and Black people.
The White people come first,
then the Colored people,
then the Black people.
Why?
Because it is so.

Next day when I met Joseph,
I smacked my chest and said:
Me, Colored!
He clapped his hands and laughed.

Joseph and I spent most
of the long summer afternoons together.
He learnt some Afrikaans from me.
I learnt some Zulu from him.
Our days were full.
There was the river to explore.
There were my swimming lessons.
I learnt to fight with sticks;
to weave a green hat
of young willow wands and leaves;
to catch frogs and tadpoles
with my hands;
to set a trap for the *springhaas;*
to make the sounds of the river birds.
There was the hot sun to comfort us.
There was the green grass to dry our bodies.
There was the soft clay with which to build.
There was the fine sand with which to fight.
There were our giant grasshoppers to race.
There were the locust swarms
when the skies turned black
and we caught them by the hundreds.
There was the rare taste of crisp,
brown-baked, salted locusts.
There was the voice of the wind in the willows.
There was the voice of the heavens
in the thunder storms.
There were the voices of two children
in laughter, ours.
There were Joseph's tales of black kings
who lived in days before the white man.

At home, I said:
Aunt Liza.
Yes?

Did we have Colored kings before the white man?
No.
Then where did we come from?
Joseph and his mother come from the
black kings who were before the white man.

Laughing and ruffling my head, she said:
You talk too much. Go'n wash up.

LONELY ROAD

Lonely road,
Not a star;
Lonely road,
Shadows far
And quiet,
Still as a dying heart.
Softly falling,
Sadly dropping,
Lonely road and you.
Shadows,
Strange dim shadows,
Creeping shadows,
Beat on the prison'd soul.
Sadness—sadness,
Bitter sadness,
That's the road I go.

Ezekiel Mphahlele

EXILE IN NIGERIA

Northern Wind
sweeping down from the Sahara
flings a grey scarf round me on and off.
The car torpedoes through the smoky haze:
I wonder what you do to my interior—
burning dry the mucus
piercing
scouring
my lungs—
savage harmattan!

Northern Wind
filtering
through tree and grass and me,
you hear my windows open
with a creak of hinges—
windows that were shut so long,
oh, so long
in the painful south of the south,
and you laugh at me—
rollicking harmattan!

Northern Wind
smelling of what I cannot smell
reminding me of things I can't or daren't remember,
what is it you do to me?
If it's remaining embers your
wasted fingers
fumble for
or violence

you're whipping me into,
groping
among slumbering drives of long ago down
in the cellar of the brain—
ah, save your breath;
I feel a certain void
now my enemies are out of sight;
only distant sound of long-tongued hounds
I hear
across the Congo and Zambesi and Limpopo
down in the painful south of the south,
and my anger
is a sediment
in the pit of my stomach
waiting
for Time's purgative or agitation—
harrowing harmattan!

Northern wind
all I know
is that you numb and jolt me
lash the water off my flesh
and fill me with a sense of insufficiency,
vague longings and forlorn moments and
brittle promises—maddening!
Twelve months I heard of you
there in the humid side of your native sands
where heat
oozed
from under me,
denuded
some of the lump of southern pain:
you did not come
I came so far to meet you.
Yesterday I watched the leaves
go fluttering

down
down
to kiss the ground before your majesty—
pretentious thing!

Northern wind
now whimpering
whining
now lisping
dead prophecies
collected from ruins of lost empires,
you weave
knotted fingers
through tree and grass and me
blowing down the serest:
stop,
tremble
when you see the savage green of us
beyond the touch of you!
Not like the lusty August winds
of the vibrant painful south of the south,
spinning us into
desperate tears and laughter
anger, hope—
blistering interlace—
still pushing us on to hell or heaven,
we running fighting running,
straining
like a universe of bending reeds.
Rather that,
northern wind,
than the long hours of sleep,
oh, so long,
that make a yawning descant
to your impotent howling,
the long mental sleep

that knows no longing
for even the now unattainable,
no unfulfilled urges
heartburns and lingering angers,
no fires kindled by wanton men
beaten out
in psychotic panic
left smouldering smouldering smouldering
in the Negro heart
in the agitated painful south of the south.
When will you stifle
this yawn of ancient languors
in the range of your compass—
indifferent harmattan?

Northern wind
while I've been talking
I've become aware of one thing
I had only surmised
since I left the
palpitating painful south of the south
they've done it to me—
taught me the violence,
revenge of Europe,
uncivilized me
by the law of
paper
gun
baton,
made me lie to them and smile,
made me think that
anger and bitterness
and running fighting running
were man's vital accessories.
Now here I fume and dig and paw the earth,
bellow

poised panting like a bull for the encounter and—
ah, no visible foe,
resistance none,
no dazzling red;
Ah the aching void in me,
neutralized acidity of my slime!
Now you know
the unsteady fulcrum of an immigrant!
Tell me,
is this divine indolence—
this
the horizontal sleep of the north?
the secret of the urge to be
only to be?
or just the great immensity of Northern Sleep?
Is it Tao's sweet narcotic wisdom—
spirit of harmattan?

Northern wind
you know nothing.
Only, since morning
I've ridden layer after layer of grey
my nose is dry
your load trapped in my hair.
You've followed me all day
relentlessly
into the catacomb of night
and still I feel
the unholy hounds of the
bleeding painful south of the south
chasing after me,
you flapping about my head
gyrating like a pack of idiots
in and out between the running wheels—
Enough!
I shan't be wooed:

Shelley's long long dead,
no messages thrown to the winds anymore
Enough
of dehydrated kisses,
barren maid,
no night club this!
But now I think of it
I'll stop at the roadhouse here
for a beer
just for a while—
the immigrant's journey's a long long one,
heavy.
He tunnels through
back again
beneath
pounding footsteps of three decades and more of hurt
on the beaten road above
weighing down
down on him.
When I burst into the dawn of brooding questions
I shall yet look at more butterflies, moths and leaves
you nailed
on my radiator
like a lover of curios who wants his pieces
dead and flat.
Morning!
New dawn tells me
that void can never last,
for the immigrant's journey's a long long road.
Over centuries
they scrambled
for my mother
from across the frontiers of snowbound boredom
decay
stale wines and bodies,
clawed down her green innocence

mauled her limbs
sold her shyness
planted
brass and wooden crosses
knocked them down at skittles
gaming for the land
while hungry eyes transfixed on a miracle
high on Calvary.
I'm a leopard
born of
a Mother
a God in torment,
converging point of centuries of change,
a continent of test-tubes.
My claws have poison:
only let me lie down a while,
bide my time,
rub my neck and whiskers,
file my claws and remember.
Then my mind can draw the line between
the hounds and hunted of the lot
in the blazing painful south of the south;
use their tools and brains—
thanks for once to ways of white folk.
And in yonder land of peace and calm,
you think I'll change my spots?
No matter,
no regrets:
the God of Africa
my Mother
will know her friends and persecutors, civilize the world
and teach them the riddle of living and dying.
Meantime,
let them leave my heart alone!

Richard Rive

WHERE THE RAINBOW ENDS

Where the rainbow ends
There's going to be a place, brother,
Where the world can sing all sorts of songs,
And we're going to sing together, brother,
You and I, though you're white and I'm not.
It's going to be a sad song, brother,
Because we don't know the tune,
And it's a difficult tune to learn.
But we can learn, brother, you and I.
There's no such tune as a black tune.
There's no such tune as a white tune.
There's only music, brother,
And it's music we're going to sing
Where the rainbow ends.

A Portuguese-speaking Poet

MOZAMBIQUE

Valente Malangatana

WOMAN

In the cool waters of the river
we shall have fish that are huge
which shall give the sign of
the end of the world perhaps
because they make an end of woman
woman who adorns the fields
woman who is the fruit of man.

The flying fish makes an end of searching
because woman is the gold of man
when she signs she even seems
like the fado-singer's well-tuned guitar
when she dies, I shall cut off
her hair to deliver me from sin.

Woman's hair shall be the blanket
over my coffin when another Artist
calls me to Heaven to paint me
Woman's breasts shall be my pillow
woman's eye shall open up for me the way to heaven
woman's belly shall give birth to me up there
and woman's glance shall watch me
as I go up to Heaven.

DOROTHY GUEDES / PHILIPPA RUMSEY

TO THE ANXIOUS MOTHER

Into your arms I came
when you bore me, very anxious
you, who were so alarmed
at that monstrous moment
fearing that God might take me.
Everyone watched in silence
to see if the birth was going well
everyone washed their hands
to be able to receive the one who came from Heaven
and all the women were still and afraid.
But when I emerged
from the place where you sheltered me so long
at once I drew my first breath
at once you cried out with joy
the first kiss was my grandmother's.
And she took me at once to the place
where they kept me, hidden away
everyone was forbidden to enter my room
because everyone smelt bad
and I all fresh, fresh
breathed gently, wrapped in my napkins.
But grandmother, who seemed like a madwoman,
always looking and looking again
because the flies came at me
and the mosquitoes harried me.
God who also watched over me
was my old granny's friend.

DOROTHY GUEDES / PHILIPPA RUMSEY

French-speaking Poets

MADAGASCAR

CONGO

SENEGAL

Jean-Joseph Rabéarivelo

FLUTE PLAYERS

Your flute
    you carved from the shinbone of a mighty bull
    and polished it on barren hills beaten by sun.

His flute
    he carved from a reed trembling in the breeze
    and cut in it little holes beside a flowing brook
    drunk on dreams of moonlight.

Together
    you made music in the late afternoon
    as if to hold back the round boat
    sinking on the shores of the sky
    to save it from its fate:
    but are your plaintive incantations
    heeded by the gods of the wind,
    of the earth, of the forest, and the sand?

Your flute
    throws out a beat like the march of an angry bull
    toward the desert—
    but who comes back running,

burned by thirst and hunger
and defeated by weariness
at the foot of a shadeless tree
with neither leaves nor fruit.

His flute
is like a reed that bends
beneath the weight of a passing bird in flight—
not a bird captured by a child
whose feathers are caressed,
but a bird lost from other birds
who looks at his own shadow for solace
in the flowing water.

Your flute and his
regret their beginnings
in the songs of both your sorrows.

LANGSTON HUGHES

HERE SHE STANDS

Here she stands
Her eyes reflecting crystals of sleep
Her eyelids heavy with timeless dreams
Her feet are rooted in the ocean
And when she lifts her dripping hands
They hold corals and shimmering salt.

She will pile them into little heaps
Close to the bay of mist
And give them to nude sailors
Whose tongues were cut out,
Until the rains begin to fall.

Then one can no longer see her
But only her windswept hair
Like a clump of unwinding seaweed
And perhaps some grains of salt.

MIRIAM KOSHLAND

Flavien Ranaivo

LOVE SONG

Do not love me, my friend,
Like your shadow—
Shadows fade in the evening
And I will hold you
Until the cock crows.

Do not love me like pepper—
It makes my belly hot.
I cannot eat pepper
When I am hungry.

Do not love me like a pillow—
One would meet in sleep
And not see each other
During the day.

Love me like a dream—
For dreams are your life
In the night
And my hope in the day.

MIRIAM KOSHLAND

Tchicaya U Tam'si

DEBOUT

excerpt

. . . . here is the stream again under the rainbow
the stream takes me by the feet and the head
the jackals are like my teeth
they stink of the knowing serpent
in one of my memory's holes
the owl watches me take
my first steps drunk with so many stars

my life is one that kills
take it
        not to die
I realize that my congo
wants to live free
freedom for
        my teeth
to be jackals
        redolent
any apple will do
if love is sad

night will come my soul is ready

E. S. YNTEMA

Patrice Emery Lumumba

DAWN IN THE HEART OF AFRICA

For a thousand years, you, African, suffered like a beast,
Your ashes strewn to the wind that roams the desert.
Your tyrants built the lustrous, magic temples
To preserve your soul, preserve your suffering.
Barbaric right of fist and the white right to a whip,
You had the right to die, you also could weep.
On your totem they carved endless hunger, endless bonds,
And even in the cover of the woods a ghastly cruel death
Was watching, snaky, crawling to you
Like branches from the holes and heads of trees
Embraced your body and your ailing soul.
Then they put a treacherous big viper on your chest:
On your neck they laid the yoke of fire-water,
They took your sweet wife for glitter of cheap pearls,
Your incredible riches that nobody could measure.
From your hut, the tom-toms sounded into dark of night
Carrying cruel laments up mighty black rivers
About abused girls, streams of tears and blood,
About ships that sailed to countries where the little man
Wallows in an anthill and where the dollar is king,
To that damned land which they called a motherland.
There your child, your wife were ground, day and night
In a frightful, merciless mill, crushing them in dreadful pain.
You are a man like others. They preach you to believe
That good white God will reconcile all men at last.
By fire you grieved and sang the moaning songs
Of a homeless beggar that sinks at strangers' doors.
And when a craze possessed you
And your blood boiled through the night
You danced, you moaned, obsessed by father's passion.

Like fury of a storm to lyrics of a manly tune
From a thousand years of misery a strength burst out of you
In metallic voice of jazz, in uncovered outcry
That thunders through the continent like gigantic surf.
The whole world surprised, wakes up in panic
To the violent rhythm of blood, to the violent rhythm of jazz,
The white man turning pallid over this new song
That carries torch of purple through the dark of night.

The dawn is here, my brother! Dawn! Look in our faces,
A new morning breaks in our old Africa.
Ours alone will now be the land, the water, mighty rivers
Poor African surrendered for a thousand years.
Hard torches of the sun will shine for us again
They'll dry the tears in eyes and spittle on your face.
The moment when you break the chains, the heavy fetters,
The evil, cruel times will go never to come again.
A free and gallant Congo will arise from black soil,
A free and gallant Congo—black blossom from black seed!

Léopold Sédar-Senghor

WE DELIGHTED, MY FRIEND

We delighted, my friend, in an African presence:
Furniture from Guinea and the Congo,
Heavy and polished, dark and light.
Primitive and pure masks on distant walls yet so near.
Taborets of honor for the hereditary hosts,
The princes from the high country.
Wild and proud perfumes from the thick tresses of silence,
Cushions of shadow and leisure like quiet wells running.
Eternal words and the distant alternating chant
As in the loin cloth from the Sudan.
But then the friendly light of your blue kindness
Will soften the obsession of this presence in
Black, white, and red, O red like the soil of Africa.

MIRIAM KOSHLAND

NIGHT OF SINE

Woman, rest on my brow your balsam hands,
Your hands gentler than fur.

The tall palm trees swinging in the night wind
Hardly rustle. Not even cradlesongs.
The rhythmic silence rocks us.
Listen to its song, listen to the beating of our dark blood, listen,
To the beating of the dark pulse of Africa in the midst of
lost villages.
Now the tired moon sinks towards its bed of slack water,
Now the peals of laughter even fall asleep, and the
bards themselves
Dandle their heads like children on the backs of their mothers.
Now the feet of the dancers grow heavy
And heavy grows the tongue of the singers.
This is the hour of the stars and of the night that dreams
And reclines on this hill of clouds, draped in her long gown
of milk.
The roofs of the houses gleam gently.
What are they telling so confidentially to the stars?
Inside the hearth is extinguished in the intimacy of bitter
and sweet scents.
Woman, light the lamp of clear oil, and let the children
In bed talk about their ancestors, like their parents.
Listen to the voice of the ancients of Elissa. Like we, exiled,
They did not want to die, lest their seminal flood be lost
in the sand.
Let me listen in the smoky hut for the shadowy visit of
propitious souls,
My head on your breast glows like a kuskus ball smoking
out of the fire,
Let me breathe the smell of our dead,
Let me contemplate and repeat their living voice, let me learn
To live before I sink, deeper than the diver, into the lofty
depth of sleep.

ULLI BEIER

SONGS FOR A THREE-STRING GUITAR (KHALAM)

I

I walked with you as far as the graineries beside the gates
of the night
And I was speechless before the golden riddle of your smile.
A fleeting twilight fell upon your face like some divine caprice.
From the top of the hill in the waning light I saw the shimmer
of your loincloth paling
And the crest of your hair like a sun sinking in the shade
of the ricefields,
When more treacherous than panthers anguish and ancestral
fears assailed me
Which my soul could not dispel beyond the day's horizon.
Will this then be the last night, the departure forever?
I shall weep in the darkness, in the maternal hollow of the earth
I shall sleep in the silence of my tears
Until my forehead again be brushed by the milky dawn
of your lips.

II

Be not astonished, my love, if at times my song grows dark
If I change my melodious reed for the khalam and the tama's beat
And the green smell of the ricefields for galloping rumble
of the tabalas.
Listen to the threats of old sorcerers, to the thundering wrath
of God!
Ah, maybe tomorrow the purple voice of your song-maker
will be silent forever
That's why today my song is so urgent and my fingers bleed
on my khalam.

Tomorrow perhaps, my love, I may fall on embattled soil
Missing your sleeping eyes and the dull tom-tom of
faraway drums
Then you in the twilight will long for my burning voice
to praise your black beauty.

MIRIAM KOSHLAND

PARIS IN THE SNOW

Lord, you visited Paris on the day of your birth
Because it had become paltry and bad.
You purified it with incorruptible cold,
The white death.
This morning even the factory funnels hoisted in harmony
The white flags.
"Peace to all men of good will."
Lord, you have offered the divided world, the divided Europe,
The snow of peace.
And the rebels fired their fourteen hundred cannons
Against the mountains of your peace.
Lord, I have accepted your white cold that burns worse than salt.
And now my heart melts like snow in the sun.
And I forget
The white hands that loaded the guns that destroyed
the kingdoms.
The hands that whipped the slaves and that whipped you
The dusty hands that slapped you, the white powdered hands
that slapped me
The sure hands that pushed me into solitude and hatred
The white hands that felled the high forest that dominated
Africa,
That felled the Sara, erect and firm in the heart of Africa,

Beautiful like the first men that were created by your own
brown hands.
They felled the virgin forest to turn into railway sleepers.
They felled Africa's forest in order to save civilization that was
lacking in men.
Lord, I can still not abandon this last hate, I know it,
The hatred of diplomats who show their long teeth
And who will barter with black flesh tomorrow.
My heart, oh lord has melted like the snow on the roofs of Paris
In the sun of your Goodness,
It is kind to my enemies, my brothers with the snowless
white hands,
Also because of the hands of dew that lie on my burning cheeks
at night.

ULLI BEIER

TO NEW YORK

for jazz orchestra: trumpet solo

I

New York! At first I was confused by your beauty, by those
great golden long-legged girls.
So shy at first before your metallic eyes, your frosted smile
So shy. And the anguish in the depths of skyscraper streets
Lifting eyes hawkhooded to the sun's eclipse.
Sulphurous your light and livid the towers with heads that
thunderbolt the sky
The skyscrapers which defy the storms with muscles of steel
and stone-glazed hide.
But two weeks on the bare sidewalks of Manhattan
At the end of the third week the fever seizes you with the pounce
of a leopard

Two weeks without rivers or fields, all the birds of the air
Falling sudden and dead on the high ashes of flat roof-tops.
No smile of a child blooms, his hand refreshed in my hand,
No mother's breast, but only nylon legs. Legs and breasts that
have not sweat nor smell.
No tender word for there are no lips, only artificial hearts
paid for in hard cash
And no book where wisdom may be read. The painter's palette
blossoms with crystals of coral.
Nights of insomnia oh nights of Manhattan! So agitated by
flickering lights, while motor horns howl of empty hours
And while dark waters carry away hygienic loves, like rivers
flooded with the corpses of children.

II

Now is the time of signs and of reckonings
New York! Now is the time of manna and hyssop.
You must but listen to the trombones of God, let your heart beat
in the rhythm of blood, your blood.
I saw in Harlem humming with noise with stately colours
and flamboyant smells
It was tea-time at the house of the seller of pharmaceutical
products—
I saw preparing the festival of night for escape from the day. I
proclaim night more truthful than the day.
It was the pure hour when in the streets God makes the life
that goes back beyond memory spring up
All the amphibious elements shining like suns.
Harlem Harlem! Now I saw Harlem! A green breeze of corn
springs up from the pavements ploughed by the
naked feet of dancers
Buttocks waves of silk, and sword blade breasts, water-lily
ballets and fabulous masks.
At the feet of police horses roll the mangoes of love
from low houses.

And I saw along the sidewalks streams of white run streams
of black milk in the blue fog of cigars.
I saw the sky in the evening snow cotton-flowers and seraphim's
wings and sorcerers' plumes.
Listen New York! Oh listen to your male voice of brass vibrating
with oboes, the anguish choked with tears falling
in great clots of blood
Listen to the distant beating of your nocturnal heart, rhythm and
blood of the tom-tom, tom-tom blood and tom-tom.

III

New York! I say to you: New York! let black blood flow into
your blood
That it may rub the rust from your steel joints, like an oil of life
That it may give to your bridges the bend of buttocks and the
suppleness of creepers.
Now return the most ancient times, the unity recovered, the
reconciliation of the Lion, the Bull and the Tree
Thoughts linked to act, ear to heart, sign to sense.
There are your rivers murmuring with scented crocodiles and
mirage-eyed manatees. And no need to invent the Sirens.
But it is enough to open eyes to the rainbow of April
And the ears, above all the ears, to God who out of the laugh of
a saxophone created the heaven and the earth in six days.
And the seventh day he slept the great sleep of the Negro.

ULLI BEIER

David Diop

THOSE WHO LOST EVERYTHING

Brightly shone the sun in my hut
And my wives were beautiful and supple

Like palm trees in the sweet breeze of evening.
My children glided on a great river
Into the depths of death
And my canoes wrestled with crocodiles.
The motherly moon played for us to dance
To the deep wild rhythm of the tom-tom—
Happy tom-tom, careless tom-tom
In the bonfires of freedom.

Then one day, silence....
It seemed as if the rays of the sun
Were extinguished in my empty hut.
My wives crushed their reddened mouths
Against the thin hard lips of the
Conquerors with eyes of steel.
My children took off their peaceful nakedness
To put on a uniform of blood and iron.
Your voice was extinguished, too.
The chains of slavery cut into my heart.
Tom-toms of my nights,
Tom-toms of my fathers!

LANGSTON HUGHES

SUFFER, POOR NEGRO

Suffer, poor Negro!
The whip whistles
Whistles in sweat and blood
Across your back.

Suffer, poor Negro!
The day is long, too long
To carry white ivory
Ivory for your white Master.

Suffer, poor Negro!
Your children are hungry
Hungry and your hut empty
Empty of your wife who sleeps
Sleeps on the Master's couch.

Suffer, poor Negro
Negro black as Misery!

LANGSTON HUGHES

THE VULTURES

In those days
When civilization kicked us in the face
When holy water slapped our tamed foreheads
The vultures built in the shadow of their talons
The blood stained monument of tutelage.
In those days
There was painful laughter on the metallic hell of the roads
And the monotonous rhythm of the paternoster
Drowned the howling on the plantations.
O the bitter memories of extorted kisses
Of promises broken at the point of a gun
Of foreigners who did not seem human,
Who knew all the books but did not know love.
But we whose hands fertilize the womb of the earth
In spite of your songs of pride
In spite of the desolate villages of torn Africa
Hope was preserved in us, as in a fortress,
And from the mines of Swaziland to the factories of Europe
Spring will be reborn under our bright steps.

ULLI BEIER

YOUR PRESENCE

In your presence I rediscovered my name
My name that was hidden under the pain of separation
I rediscovered the eyes, no longer veiled with fever
And your laughter, like a flame piercing the shadows,
Has revealed Africa to me, beyond the snows of yesterday.
Ten years, my love
With days of illusions and shattered ideas
And sleep made restless with alcohol
Ten years inhaling the suffering of the world
The suffering that burdens today with the taste of tomorrow
And that turns love into a boundless river
In your presence I have rediscovered the memory of my blood
And necklaces of laughter hung around our days
Days sparkling with new joys.

ULLI BEIER

AFRICA

Africa, my Africa,
Africa of proud warriors
In ancestral savannas,
Africa of whom my grandmother sings,
On the banks of the distant river
I have never known you
But your blood flows in my veins
Your beautiful black blood
That irrigates the fields
The blood of your sweat
The work of your slavery
The slavery of your children.
Africa, tell me, Africa,
Is this you, this back that is bent,
This back that breaks
Under the weight of humiliation
This back trembling with red scars
Saying *yes* to the whip under the midday sun?
A grave voice answers me:
Impetuous son, this tree, young and strong,
This tree there in splendid islolation
Amidst white and faded flowers,
That is Africa, your Africa,
That grows again, patiently, obstinately
As its fruit gradually acquires
The bitter taste of liberty.

ULLI BEIER

BIOGRAPHICAL NOTES

BIOGRAPHICAL NOTES

PETER ABRAHAMS was born in 1919 in the slums of Johannesburg, South Africa, and lived there until he was twenty. Then for a time he worked as a stoker at sea, but soon thereafter he began to earn his living as a writer, and continues to do so to this day. As a refugee from apartheid, he lived in England with his wife and children, but when in the 1950's he was sent to the West Indies on a writing assignment, he fell in love with Jamaica and is now settled there, working as a free lance journalist. As Africa's most famous writer of color, his books include novels, reportage, and a brilliant autobiography, *Tell Freedom*, which has been described as "the mirror of life in a tragic land."

GEORMBEEYI ADALI-MORTTI of Ghana is an interpreter and translator of Ewe poetry as well as a writer of English verse. Before leaving Accra with his wife and three daughters for an extended sojourn in the United States as a graduate student at Cornell, he was one of the founders of the literary magazine, *Okyeame*, published by the Ghana Society of Writers.

FRANK ABIODUN AIG-IMOUKHUEDE, born near Ife, Benin Province, Nigeria, in 1935, was graduated from the University College, Ibadan. Of Yoruba parentage, his father, a clergyman, died just before completing a translation of the New Testament into Ora, a widely spoken Bini dialect. At college where Frank majored in English, he wrote two plays for campus production. He was later employed in radio at Broadcasting House in Lagos, then as a reporter on the *Daily Express*. Now he is with the Ministry of Information at Ibadan. Much of his verse is in pidgin-English, the *lingua franca* of West Africa. Its dialect possesses an urban folk flavor full of earthy humor, but is difficult for foreigners to understand. Aig-Imoukhuede delights in remaining close to the people.

"Wetin you git wey your head dey swell?" one of his poems asks—which means, "How far can you go if you get the big head?"

EDWIN BARCLAY was Secretary of State and then for twelve years the President of Liberia. He was the first Liberian head of government to travel extensively in the jungles of the back country, taking a personal interest in the various tribes and their lore. Barclay did much writing and authored his country's national anthem, *The Lone Star Forever*. Shortly before his death in 1953, he visited the United States.

ULLI BEIER (Horst Ulrich Beier) of German parentage is a long-time resident of Nigeria, a lecturer on African literature at University College, Ibadan, a distinguished translator of the myths and songs of the Yoruba people, and co-editor of the literary magazine, *Black Orpheus*. Beier's wife, Suzanne Wenger, an Austrian born artist and anthropologist, has become a Priestess of a secret Yoruba cult near Oshogbo, and Beier himself often wears the native *agbada* dress. He is one of the founders of Mbari, an organization of artists and writers with headquarters at Ibadan. Beier's recent book, *Yoruba Poetry*, is published by the Ministry of Education.

KWESI BREW, born in 1928 at Cape Coast, was recipient of a British Council Poetry Prize while a student at the University College of Ghana. He is now in the Ghana Foreign Service. Of a convivial nature, Brew is often considered "the life of the party" at gatherings of Accra's diplomatic and literary circles.

JOHN PEPPER CLARK, during his student years at Ibadan, was the founder and editor of a literary magazine, *The Horn*. He is now the leading editorial writer on the Lagos *Daily Express*. Clark comes from the "river people" of the Niger Delta and bears three tiny cast marks beside his eyes and four on each cheek, as is the custom of his tribe. In 1962 he came to the United States as a graduate student at Princeton.

PETER CLARKE, whose pen name was formerly Kumalo, is a resident of Simon's Town, Cape Province, South Africa. He has been a dock worker, but now devotes most of his time to painting and writing. He illustrated the German edition of Alan Paton's *Too Late The Phalarope* as well as a collection of Ezekiel Mphahlele's stories published in Nigeria. Clarke's paintings, drawings, and block prints have been exhibited in leading South African galleries, including the National Gallery at the Cape, and his poems and stories have appeared in various African and European publications.

J. B. DANQUAH (Joseph Boakye Danquah) was born in 1895 in Bepons, Ghana, then called the Gold Coast. He became a lawyer but devoted much of his time to political opposition to colonialism. In 1947 he founded his country's first nationalist party, the United Gold Coast Convention, and offered the position of Secretary General to Kwame Nkrumah. Dr. Danquah has experienced both exile and imprisonment for his political activities, and is leader of the opposition to the Nkrumah government. A leading authority on Akan-Ashanti laws and customs, Danquah is the author of many poems and a play, *The Third Woman*, in which his vast knowledge of folklore and folk songs is utilized for the theatre.

MICHAEL F. DEI-ANANG, author of a collection of poems, *Africa Speaks*, and the play, *Cocoa Comes to Mampong*, is a former senior government official of the Ghana Ministry of Foreign Affairs, but now has been elevated to the rank of Ambassador Plenipotentiary and Minister Extraordinary.

ROLAND TOMBEKAI DEMPSTER, one of the founders of the Society of Liberian Authors in Monrovia, was educated at Liberia College. He later studied journalism in the United States, returning to his native land to become Editor-in-Chief of *The Liberian Age*. He has taught at the University of Liberia, has published books of both poetry and prose, and is now engaged in compiling an anthology of Liberian poetry.

DAVID DIOP was born in 1927 at Bordeaux and lived most of his life as a semi-invalid in France, although a brief portion of his childhood was spent in Senegal and the Cameroons, the lands of his father and mother respectively. His first volume of poems, *Coups de Pilon*, was published in Paris. His second manuscript of poems was lost in a plane crash over the Atlantic in which Diop and his wife died in 1960.

ADEBAYO FALETI is a young Yoruba poet and specialist in the folklore of the Nigerian people. He is currently a script writer on the staff of Television House in Ibadan, the largest black city in the world. His poem "Independence" won First Award for Yoruba Literature in the 1957 Western Nigeria Festival of the Arts.

F. KWASI FIAWOO of Ewe parentage was the founder and became the first president of the New Africa University College at Anloga,

Ghana. He himself translated his play, *The Fifth Landing Stage*, from Ewe into English. Published in 1943 in London, a publisher's note states, "Only yesterday we were thinking of an Africa of fable, drum and dance. . . . Gesture in varying rhythm accompanied by sound in appropriate tones—whether of drum or of choral ejaculation—told the story and pictured the scene. Today Africa . . . does not desert the drum or the dance. She experiments in a new technique. It is drama upon which she is still busy: now with literary articulation."

MARINA GASHE is the pen name of Mrs. Elimo Njau. She and her husband are both teachers. Of the Kikuyu tribe, from Kenya, Marina Gashe studied at Makerere College in Uganda. In 1960 her first play, *The Scar*, won a drama festival award at the National Theatre in Kampala. Her husband is a Chakko painter from the slopes of Kilimanjaro in Tanganyika. They are the parents of one child and live in Kampala.

ROLF ITALIAANDER, a Hollander now living in Germany, has traveled widely in Africa and is a collector of its art and folklore. His books, including *The New Leaders of Africa*, are published in Europe and America, and he has lectured at many colleges in the United States.

K. B. JONES-QUARTEY has studied and traveled in the United States, and is married to an American. He is now Director of Extra Mural Studies at the University of Ghana and a Member of the Ghana Society of Writers.

A. C. JORDAN, born in 1906, was for a number of years a lecturer on Bantu languages at the School of African Studies of the University of Cape Town, but is now in California on a fellowship. He is a distinguished translator from the Xhosa and other native tongues, in one of which he has written a novel translated into English as *The Wrath of the Ancestors*.

ELLIS AYITEY KOMEY of the Ga tribe, Ghana, is now editor of the magazine, *Flamingo*, in London where he has lived as a journalist for many years. In 1962 Mr. Komey toured the United States.

MIRIAM KOSHLAND, German born, has lived in various parts of the world, including San Francisco, but is now a resident of Peru. She has published many translations of African and Afro-Caribbean poetry.

KOJO GYINAYE KYEI of Ghana, whose birth date was never recorded, was born sometime during the early thirties in Ahafo, Ashanti, and was educated in Catholic schools. He received a diploma from St. Augustine's College, Cape Coast. In 1956, on a scholarship from Accra's Cocoa Marketing Board, he came to study architecture at the University of Kansas. Still in the United States, Kyei has recently been teaching the Twi language to Peace Corps members studying for service in Ghana.

AQUAH LALUAH (Gladys May Casely-Hayford), born in 1904 of a distinguished Fanti family at Axim on the Gold Coast, was educated in England. Her first poems were published in the *Atlantic Monthly*. She was a teacher in Sierra Leone where she died in 1950.

PATRICE EMERY LUMUMBA, the first Premier of the strife-torn Republic of the Congo, was reported to have been assassinated by political opponents in February, 1961, at the age of thirty-five. In death he gained immortality throughout the African continent as a symbol of Pan-Africanism. His one book, *Congo, My Country*, was published posthumously.

VALENTE GOENHA MALANGATANA was born in the Portuguese East African village of Marracuene in Mozambique in 1936 and remembers that his mother did bead work and tattooing on stomachs and faces and also knew how to sharpen teeth. His father worked in the mines of South Africa. Valente took a very early interest in drawing and painting but had little encouragement until, when he was 23, an architect in Lourenço Marques offered him a studio and an allowance so that he might paint without worry. "I love art and poetry," writes Malangatana. "Poetry is art written on white paper without color and in repeated letters, but poetry in a picture has life, smell and movement also." His first one-man show of strange and highly individual painting caused him to be hailed as one of the most promising of "an exciting new generation of African artists."

A. L. MILNER-BROWN is a free-lance writer, newspaper man and teacher living in Accra.

BLOKE MODISANE, writer and actor, has appeared in *The Blacks* and other plays in London. He is now living in England as a refugee from apartheid, having escaped from South Africa on foot without a passport to Tanganyika, thence to Europe. Looking at his newborn babe in Johannesburg just before he left, he felt a pang of remorse, he said, "for bringing such innocence into the world to perpetuate the work of the devil." Modisane contributes articles and fiction to various magazines and has completed an autobiographical narrative.

EZEKIEL MPHAHLELE, born in 1919 in South Africa, was in his childhood a tribal herd boy. As a young man he worked on the magazine, *Drum,* a picture publication devoted primarily to subjects of interest to black Africans. Fleeing apartheid, Mphahlele and his wife and three children settled in Nigeria where he taught at the University College. They now live in Paris where he is executive secretary of the Congress for Cultural Freedom. His books include an autobiography, *Down Second Avenue*, a volume of short stories, *The Living and the Dead*, and *The African Image.*

CHUBA NWEKE is in charge of the offices of the London and Kano Trading Company in Lagos, the father of one child and an avid reader of American poetry and prose. Much of his verse, a mixture of pidgin and standard English, is not readily understandable to non-African readers.

ABIOSEH NICOL, Sierra Leone, was educated in Nigeria and Sierra Leone. He later studied at British Universities. He was awarded the Margaret Wrong Prize and Medal for Literature in Africa in 1952. His short stories, articles, and poems have appeared in numerous English publications.

GABRIEL IMOMOTIMI OBAINBAING OKARA, who is considered by many to be the outstanding Nigerian poet, translates the folklore of his Ijaw heritage. Awaiting the publication of his first novel, he is serving as press officer of the Nigerian Information Service at Enugu. Okara has read his poems in various countries of Africa, in Europe and the United States, and his poems have been translated into several languages including Hebrew.

CHRISTOPHER OKIGBO, born at Ojoto in Eastern Nigeria in 1932, majored in Classical Languages at University College, Ibadan, and after graduation became vice-principal of a high school there, then Librarian of the University of Nigeria at Nsukka. He is now representative of the Cambridge University Press in Nigeria. Okigbo has published two books of poems, *Heavensgate* and *The Limits and Other Poems.*

ANDREW AMANKWA OPOKU, born in 1912 in Ashanti, is the son of a Presbyterian minister. He taught school until 1951 when he became Twi editor for the Bureau of Ghana Languages. Recently he accepted a position with Radio Ghana as a multi-lingual announcer and consultant on literary programs for popular consumption. He spent some months in Australia studying communications.

DENNIS CHUKUDE OSADEBAY, born at Asaba, Nigeria, is a member of the House of Assembly in Ibadan and the author of a book of poems, *Africa Sings*, published while Osadebay was a student of law in England. He writes in both Yoruba and English.

FRANCIS ERNEST KOBINA PARKES was born in Accra in 1932 of an Akan mother and received from her the name Kobina, which is given to all male Akans born on Tuesday. He was at one time president of the Ghana Society of Writers, but is now living in London. Parkes describes himself as an "ex-editor, ex-radio producer with Radio Ghana, ex-television script writer, ex-publicity man, ex-press attaché to the Ministry of Information, and one who hopes soon to be the ex-author of a volume of poetry, a collection of short stories, plays, and two autobiographies."

FRANCESCA YETUNDE PEREIRA was born in 1933 in Lagos of Brazilian repatriates, graduated from University College in London in 1959 with honors. On her return to Nigeria she joined the Federal Service as an administrative officer attached to the Cabinet. Shortly thereafter she received first prize for a short story entered in the Nigerian Broadcasting competition. A charming folk singer, Miss Pereira appeared at the American Society of African Culture Festival of the Arts in 1961 in Lagos, with the poet, Wole Soyinka, accompanying her on the guitar.

JEAN-JOSEPH RABÉARIVELO, Madagascar's most famous poet writing in French, died in Tananarive at the age of thirty-six from self-administered poison. He began his literary career in 1924 with a volume of poems called *La coupe de cendres*. In succeeding years his poems achieved wide popularity at home and abroad and his books were published in such divergent countries as Tunisia and Brazil.

FLAVIEN RANAIVO, son of the Governor of Arivonimama, was born in Madagascar in 1914. He is the author of a popular volume of poems in the folk manner, *L'Ombre et la Vent*, published in Tananarive.

RICHARD RIVE was born in District Six in the heart of Cape Town in 1931. His father was an American Negro seaman, his mother a Cape Coloured, as persons of mixed blood are commonly called. A Boy Scout in his childhood, Rive became an outstanding track star before his graduation in 1949 from the University of Cape Town. He is now a teacher of English Literature and Latin in a large high school for Coloureds. His short stories have been published in the Scandanavian countries and in Germany, and his first novel is nearing completion.

JAMES DAVID RUBADIRI was born in 1930 in Nyasaland where, after studying pedagogy at Makerere College, Uganda, and in England, he returned to become a teacher. In recent years he has been "detained" several times for agitating against colonial rule.

LÉOPOLD SÉDAR-SENGHOR, the most famous poet of French-speaking Africa, was born in Senegal in 1906. He studied at the Sorbonne and became Professor of African Languages and Civilization at the École Nationale de France until he entered politics. Formerly a representative from Senegal in the Chamber of Deputies at Paris, he is now the President of his native land. He is the author of numerous books of poems and editor of the definitive anthology of African poetry, *Le Nouvelle Poesie Negre et Malgache*. In 1961 President Senghor paid an official visit to the United States and was a guest of President Kennedy at the White House.

WOLE SOYINKA, born of Yoruba parentage in 1934 at Abeokuta, Nigeria, was educated at Government College and at Leeds University in England. For a year he was attached as a writer to the Royal Court Theatre in London where his play, *The Invention*, was staged. He is now a Research Fellow in Drama at the University College, Ibadan, where several of his plays, including *The Lion and the Jewel*, *Dance of the Forest*, and *The Swamp Dwellers*, have been presented. Soyinka has visited Australia and the United States where he inspected university theatres. He has a small preschool age son whose name is Imodoye.

TCHICAYA U TAM'SI (Gerard Felix-Tchicaya) was born in 1931 at Mpili, Central Congo. He presently lives in Paris, where he works as a free lance writer and producer-director of his own radio scripts, as well as serving as a frequent advisor for Unesco. He is the author of four books of poems, *Le Mauvais Sang*, *Feu de Brousse*, *A Trichecoeur*, and *Epitome*, as well as a novel, *Les Cancrelats*, soon to be published.

PERMISSION CREDITS

THE EDITOR is grateful to the following authors, translators, and publishers for permission to include the poems published in this anthology:

Peter Abrahams for "Me, Colored" (excerpt from *Tell Freedom*) and "Lonely Road," published in *Presence Africaine*

G. Adali-Mortti for "Palm Leaves of Childhood," published in *Okyeame*

Frank Aig-Imoukhuede for "One Wife for One Man"

The Atlantic for "The Sorrow of Kodio," "We Delighted, My Friend," and "Debout"

Ulli Beier for his translations of "Three Friends," "Oriki Erinle," "Erin," "Shango," and "Hunger," published in *Black Orpheus*

Kwesi Brew for "A Plea for Mercy," "The Search," "The Lonely Traveller," and "Ancestral Faces," published in *Okyeame*

John Pepper Clark for "Agbor Dancer," and "Fulani Cattle" from *Poems,* Mbari Publications, Ibadan

Peter Clarke for "Play Song," "Young Shepherd Bathing His Feet," and "In Air"

Cooperative Recreation Service, Inc. for "Paddling Song" and "Nana Kru," published in *African Song Sampler*

J. B. Danquah for his translation of "Foolish Child," from his play *The Third Woman*

Michael F. Dei-Anang for "My Africa"

Ronald Tombekai Dempster for "Is This Africa?" and "Africa's Plea," from his *A Song Out of Midnight*

David Diop for "Those Who Lost Everything," "Suffer, Poor Negro"; for "The Vultures," "Your Presence," and "Africa" (translated by Ulli Beier), published in *Black Orpheus*

Drum Publications for permission to reprint "O Lamb Give Me My Salt," "Pass Office Song," "Trousers of Wind," "Keep It Dark," "Shadow of Darkness," "Nativity," and "Stanley Meets Mutesa," published in *Darkness and Light*

Adebayo Faleti for "Independence"

F. Kwasi Fiawoo for "Soliloquy on Death"

Marina Gashe for "The Village"

Rolf Italiaander for his translation of "Little Bird"

K. B. Jones-Quartey for "Stranger, Why Do You Wonder So?" published in *Okyeame*

A. C. Jordan for "You Tell Me To Sit Quiet"; and for his translations of "Shaka, King of the Zulus," Thou Great God," "Absent Lover," and "Six to Six"

Ellis Ayitey Komey for "Oblivion" and "The Damage You Have Done"

Miriam Koshland for her translations of "Half Sigh" and "The Sorrow of Kodio"
Kojo Gyinaye Kyei for "The Talking Drums" and "African in Louisiana"
Valente Goenha Malangatana for "Woman" and "To the Anxious Mother" (translated by Dorothy Guedes and Philippa Rumsey)
Kweku Martin for "Prayer for Every Day," from *Voices of Ghana*, Ghana Broadcast
A. L. Milner-Brown for "Who Knows?"
Bloke Modisane for "One Thought for My Lady," "blue black," "black blues," and "Lonely"
Ezekiel Mphahlele for "Exile in Nigeria," published in *Black Orpheus*
Chuba Nweke for "Moon Song"
Abioseh Nicol for "African Easter" and "The Meaning of Africa"
Gabriel Okara for "Piano and Drums," "You Laughed and Laughed and Laughed," published in *Black Orpheus;* for "Were I To Choose," "The Call of the River Nun," "Once Upon a Time," and "To Adhiambo"
Christopher Okigbo for "Lament of the Flutes"
Andrew Amankwa Opoku for "River Afram," published in *New World Writings*
Dennis C. Osadebay for "The African Trader's Complaint," published in his book *Africa Sings*
Francis Ernest Kobina Parkes for "Three Phases of Africa," "Apocalypse," and "Blind Steersmen"
Francesca Yetunde Pereira for "The Paradox," "Mother Dark," "The Burden," and "Two Strange Worlds"
Jean-Joseph Rabéarivelo for "Flute Players" and "Here She Stands"
Flavien Ranaivo for "Love Song" (translated by Miriam Koshland)
Richard Rive for "Where the Rainbow Ends"
James David Rubadiri for "Stanley Meets Mutesa," published in *Darkness and Light*
Léopold Sédar-Senghor for "We Delighted, My Friend" (translated by Miriam Koshland), published in *The Atlantic;* "Night of Sine" and "Paris in the Snow" (translated by Ulli Beier), published in *Black Orpheus;* "To New York" (translated by Ulli Beier), in *The Twentieth Century;* and "Songs for a Three-String Guitar" (translated by Miriam Koshland)
Wole Soyinka for "Abiku"
Tchicaya U Tam'si for "Debout" (translated by E. S. Yntema), published in *The Atlantic*

Every effort has been made to locate all persons having any rights or interests in the poems published here. If some acknowledgments have not been made, their omission is unintentional.